I Am a Soldier, Too

***Also by Rick Bragg
in Large Print:***

All Over but the Shoutin'

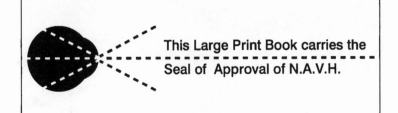

I Am a Soldier, Too

The Jessica Lynch Story

RICK BRAGG

Thorndike Press • Waterville, Maine

05 May 5
Gale
3095 (2167)

Published in 2004 by arrangement with Alfred A. Knopf, Inc.

Thorndike Press® Large Print Biography.

The tree indicium is a trademark of Thorndike Press.

The text of this Large Print edition is unabridged.
Other aspects of the book may vary from the original edition.

Set in 16 pt. Plantin by Liana M. Walker.

Printed in the United States on permanent paper.

Library of Congress Cataloging-in-Publication Data

Bragg, Rick.
    I am a soldier, too : the Jessica Lynch story / Rick Bragg.
      p. cm.
    ISBN 0-7862-6381-4 (lg. print : hc : alk. paper)
    1. Iraq War, 2003 — Personal narratives, American.
2. Lynch, Jessica, 1983– 3. Prisoners of war — United
States — Biography. 4. Prisoners of war — Iraq —
Biography. 5. Women soldiers — United States —
Biography. I. Title: Jessica Lynch story. II. Title.
DS79.76.B73 2004
956.7044′3—dc22
  [B]   2004041205

*This book is dedicated to the memory of
Private First Class Lori Piestewa,
Jessica's friend and protector,
who was killed in the ambush
at Nasiriyah on March 23, 2003.*

*It is also dedicated to the memories of the other
ten soldiers who lost their lives in the ambush:*

*Specialist Jamaal Addison
Specialist Edward Anguiano
Sergeant George Buggs
First Sergeant Robert Dowdy
Private Ruben Estrella-Soto
Private First Class Howard Johnson II
Specialist James Kiehl
Chief Warrant Officer Johnny Villareal Mata
Private Brandon U. Sloan
Sergeant Donald R. Walters*

As the Founder/CEO of NAVH, the only national health agency solely devoted to those who, although not totally blind, have an eye disease which could lead to serious visual impairment, I am pleased to recognize Thorndike Press* as one of the leading publishers in the large print field.

Founded in 1954 in San Francisco to prepare large print textbooks for partially seeing children, NAVH became the pioneer and standard setting agency in the preparation of large type.

Today, those publishers who meet our standards carry the prestigious "Seal of Approval" indicating high quality large print. We are delighted that Thorndike Press is one of the publishers whose titles meet these standards. We are also pleased to recognize the significant contribution Thorndike Press is making in this important and growing field.

Lorraine H. Marchi, L.H.D.
Founder/CEO
NAVH

* Thorndike Press encompasses the following imprints: Thorndike, Wheeler, Walker and Large Pr int Press.

Contents

Illustrations follow page 170.

Introduction

Hero

On most nights of the year, this stretch of country road is only a flat place in the dark. But for a few nights in late summer 2003, it blazed in neon, smelled like smoked sausage, spun sugar and blue-ribbon hogs, and rang with screams of people who had bought a ticket to be scared. They rode the Tilt-A-Whirl, browsed tents of prizewinning fruit preserves and lined up for the cute-baby contest, and if there is such a thing as a time machine on earth, it must be powered by the Ferris wheel at the Wirt County, West Virginia, Fair. Back from the war, Jessica Lynch asked her mother and father to take her there.

"She went every year until she left for the army," said Dee Lynch, Jessi's mother. "She would meet her friends — everybody knew everybody. It's just a little county fair. You could sit at one end of the thing and watch your kids play at the other end. It never changed."

The ping and rattle of the rides and games reached all the way to the parking lot as Greg Lynch pushed Jessi's wheelchair toward the glow of the midway, over ruts that jostled her legs (which had been repaired with a metal rod and a screw), her pieced-together arm and her back, which had been realigned with metal plates.

But she was sick of lying in her adjustable bed at home. "It was her first real public appearance," her mother said. "She wanted to see the cute-baby contest, but we never got that far."

It started with a polite, shy inquiry from an old man.

"Ma'am, can my wife stand by you while I take a picture?"

And in seconds — not minutes, but seconds — Jessi was surrounded by people who just wanted to touch her, to say hello, or just to look at her. The word trickled through the crowd — "Jessi's here" — and there was no way to move the wheelchair one inch farther.

"Can I sit my child on your lap?" one woman said, and then another asked, and another. The cameras flashed and old women hugged her shoulders or said "Bless your heart." A little girl asked, "Mommy, is that the girl from TV?" One old man told her he had lost two sons and had given up on living, but her story made him ashamed to give up.

"It was real nice and stuff," Jessi said.

Over and over again, they said the same thing to her.

"You're a hero."

The word bounced from person to person.

Hero.

An hour passed, the wheels of her chair locked in a circle of adoring people.

Hero.

"It was weird," Jessi said later, sitting at her kitchen table, her pain medication lined up in front of her beside a glass of chocolate milk. The very word makes her sad. "For twenty years, no one knew my name. Now they want my autograph. But I'm not a hero. If it makes people feel good to say it, then I'm glad. But I'm not. I'm just a survivor. When I think about it, it keeps me awake at night."

One

The Deadliest Day

SOUTHERN IRAQ
March 2003

The recruiter said she would travel. Now, twenty months after enlistment, nineteen-year-old Private First Class Jessica Lynch steered her groaning diesel truck across a hateful landscape of grating sand and sucking mud, hauling four hundred gallons of water in the rough direction of Baghdad on a mission that just felt bad. Back home, boys with tears in their eyes had offered to marry her, to build her a brand-new house, anything, to get her to stay forever in the high, green lonesome. She told them no, told them she was going to see the world.

But the recruiter had not told any lies. He offered her a way to make some money for college, so that, when this hitch was over, she could become the kindergarten teacher she wanted to be. And he offered a way to escape the inertia of the West Virginia hills, a place so beautiful that a young person can forget, sometimes until she is very old, that she is standing still. In the process, she would serve her country, something people in her part of America still say without worrying that someone will roll his eyes.

She bought it. They all had, pretty much: all the soldiers around her, the sons and daughters of endangered blue-collar workers, immigrant families and single mothers — a United States Army borrowed from tract houses, brick ranchers and back roads. The not-quite beneficiaries of trickle-down economics, they had traded uncertain futures for dead-certain paychecks and a place in the adventure that they had heard their ancestors talk of as they'd twisted wrenches, pounded IBM Selectrics and packed lunches for the plants that closed their doors before the next generation could build a life from them.

The military never closed its doors, and service was passed down like a gold pocket watch. Sometimes it was a good safe bet, all beer gardens and G.I. Bills, and sometimes it was snake eyes, and the soldiers found themselves at a Chosin Reservoir, or a Hue, or on a wrong turn to An Nasiriyah.

As the convoy of big diesels waddled across the sand, the world she saw was flat, dull and yellow-brown, except where the water had turned the dust to reddish paste. She got excited when she saw a tree. Trees made sense. She had grown up in the woods, where solid walls of hardwood had sunk roots deep into the hillsides and kept the ground pulled tight, as it should be, to the planet. All this empty space and loose, shifting sand unsettled her mind and made her feel lost, long before she found out it was true.

She was afraid. The big trucks had been breaking down since they left the base in Kuwait, giving in to the grit that ate at the moving parts or bogging down in the mud and sand like wallowing cows. Her convoy, part of the 507th Maintenance Company deployed from Fort Bliss, Texas, was at the tail end of a massive supply line that stretched from the Kuwaiti border through southern Iraq, a caravan loaded with food, fuel, water, spare parts and toilet paper. Her convoy followed the route that had already been rutted or churned up by the columns ahead, and every time a five-ton truck hit a soft place and bottomed out, the thirty-three vehicles in Jessica's convoy dropped farther behind.

Jessica just remembers a foreboding, a feeling that the convoy was staggering into enemy country without purpose or direction. Two days into the mission, the convoy had dropped so far behind that it had lost radio contact with the rest of the column. One of the far-ahead convoys carried her boyfriend, Sergeant Ruben Contreras, who had promised he would look after her. The day they left Kuwait, his column had pulled out just ahead of hers — in plain view. Now he had vanished in the distance along with the rest.

The convoy shrank every day as the heavy trucks just sank into the sand and came apart. In just two days, the thirty-three vehicles in the convoy had dwindled to eighteen, and two of them were being towed by wreckers. One day, it took five hours to lurch just nine miles. To make up that distance and time, the soldiers in the 507th slept little or not at all. They were cooks, clerks and mechanics, none of them tested in combat. They became bone weary and sleepwalked through the days.

Jessica began to wonder, if her truck broke down, would anyone even notice her at the side of the road? There was a lot to be afraid of here. But that was what she was most afraid of, whether it was reasonable or not. She was afraid of being left behind.

"I hoped that someone would see me, that someone would pick me up," she said. "Someone would stop. But you didn't know it. You didn't know."

Everyone knew what Saddam's soldiers did to women captives. In her worst nightmares, she stood alone in that desert as the trucks of her own army pulled away. In her mind, which she struggled to keep clear as the days and nights faded together, she could see the Iraqis rise up out of the sand to come and get her.

"I didn't want to be left out there. I didn't want to be left out there on my own. Even though stuff didn't look right with the convoy, it was better than being alone."

It was not a paralyzing fear, nothing that stopped her from doing her duty. It was simple dread.

Three days into their mission, as she rode with a sergeant, the transfer case in her five-ton truck "just busted" — and they were stranded. As if in her finely tailored nightmare, the big trucks did just grind past. Not all of them had working radios, only orders to push ahead, to make up the lost time. For a few bleak heartbeats, it looked as if her little-girl's fear was real. Then a Humvee swerved off the road, and the driver beckoned to her. *"Get in."* It was PFC Lori Ann Piestewa, her best friend. The sergeant hopped in another truck, and they rolled on.

A Hopi from Arizona who had been Jessica's roommate at Fort Bliss, Lori was recovering from an injured shoulder and had been given the choice of whether or not to deploy with her unit to Iraq. She went because Jessi did. A twenty-three-year-old mother of two, PFC Piestewa knew that her roommate was nervous, and she did not want her to face the desert, and war, on her own. "She stopped," said Jessica. "She picked me up. I love her."

Far ahead, Sergeant Ruben Contreras sat in his truck as it rolled across the sands, cloaked in the sense of invincibility that a machine gun tends to lend. He was twenty-three, hopelessly in love with a five-foot-three, hundred-pound waif from a little bitty place called Palestine, West Virginia, and sick with worry. He was supposed to eyeball the road, to sweep the horizon for signs of trouble, but his thoughts were tugged back along the ruts his unit had cut in the sand.

Where was she?

At least, if everything went according to plan, there was a big, big army between his girlfriend and danger. If everything went according to plan, a shooting fight along the assigned route was unlikely for the supply-line soldiers who were purposefully skirting trouble spots, including heavily defended Nasiriyah.

"If there was any comfort, it was knowing that anything that was gonna harm her was gonna have to come through me first," he said. Rumbling over the sand, the convoys had seemed like an endless train, bound for the same place, bound together.

Jessi's convoy would be fine, he tried to convince himself. The only way it could come to real harm would be if it got lost, if the officer in charge wandered off course and into the hornet's nest of fighters loyal to Saddam who still controlled the cities and towns like Nasiriyah. Such a thing could never happen.

It was not a wrong turn, merely a missed one.

The little convoy of stragglers rolled into Nasiriyah in the early morning of March 23 — right downtown.

The army, which usually does not use such colorful language in its reports, would later describe what happened next as "a torrent of fire."

When Jessica thinks about it now, she closes her eyes.

"They were blowing us up."

The Iraqis fired point-blank into the trucks with rocket-propelled grenades, shattering metal and glass, shredding tires. Soldiers leapt from them and were shot down by Iraqis with AK-47 assault rifles who swarmed across rooftops and leaned from windows. A tank rattled up, its cannon tracking toward the trucks that growled and swerved through the dust and smoke, but the convoy was already in ruins. Some U.S. soldiers raced to cover and fought back; others clawed frantically at M16s that had jammed from the grime. Inside the Humvee with Lori, a sergeant and two other soldiers, Jessica watched bullets punch through the windshield, and she lowered her head to her knees, shut her eyes and began to pray.

It was a slow Sunday, winding down from a slow Saturday, in Palestine, West Virginia. Cody, the old dog that had never been quite the same after being shot by a hunter some years before, played dead on the front porch. Inside the white A-frame house that had been built on a foundation of hundred-year-old logs, Deadra and Greg Lynch, Jessi's parents, watched the television news. In the afternoon, CNN said a maintenance convoy had been ambushed. The network showed a video image of a truck, its doors blown away, blood running down its side. CNN said it was the 507th, and Greg told Dee not to panic, even as something like an icepick gouged at his chest. But people here have sat up late with a lot of wars, and they know that the army usually tells bad news in person. As darkness dropped on the hollow, the only visitors were friends and kin, as word spread as if by magic through the trees that one of their own was in peril.

About 11:15 p.m., a friend called from the door, "There's a trooper car comin'."

A state trooper and another man, in an army uniform, got out of the car and walked up the drive.

Dee screamed.

Like her daughter, she just wanted to hide, to make it go away.

So she just ran, as fast as she could, barefoot on the cold rocks, into the dark.

Two

Princess

Her bangs were always perfect.

Radiant in her burgundy form-hugging gown, she was crowned Miss Congeniality at the 2000 Wirt County Fair. Even the steer she raised took a ribbon that year, a good year, her last at Wirt County High. Her sister and brother called her, with only a little meanness, the princess, and she reigned over a mountain landscape that reached all the way from Singing Hills to Reedy Creek. Here, she learned to drive on roads that twisted like a snake on fire, guiding her mom's Toyota 4×4 pickup through places like Mingo Bottom, Lucille, Blue Goose and Folly Run, past plywood

21

placards that offered molasses for eight dollars a quart and church marquees that promised everlasting life. In time, it all became so familiar that she barely saw it anymore, barely noticed the letters painted on century-old barns and roadside signs that begged passersby to REMEMBER ROD WITH LOVE, or CHEW MAIL POUCH TOBACCO, or the puzzling PINCH YORSELF — IF YOU FEEL IT, IT AIN'T JESUS. It is the place where she walked a swinging bridge to see her late great-grandpa, where she played popgun soldier in the deep woods with her baby sister and her older brother, who chewed the feet off her Barbie dolls. This is where she broke her arm on the playground slide and broke David Huber's second-grade heart, where she crashed into the right-field fence after fly balls, dove onto the hardwood gym floor after loose balls, then got up and adjusted her socks.

Her kin believe she is alive, in part, because she is from this place, because she has the right blood in her. They know that doctors in three countries brought her back from near-death, that soldiers rescued her as her wounds festered, that millions prayed. Still, even though she is small and a little prissy, she carries the blood of the mountains — the blood of people who fought and worked and loved here. Even if it is not a thing that anyone can prove, it makes people glad to believe it. If that is a bad thing, then what are legends for?

Her family has lived here for going on two centuries now, farming the bottomland and raising cattle and horses, or working factory jobs in the small industrial cities that dot the mountains just east of the Ohio River. Like most people here, her people do not see themselves as Southern or Northern, just By God West Virginian — in a state so conflicted during the Civil War that sometimes nothing more than a wooden fence divided sympathies, and brothers really did kill brothers. It is still a land of feuds, where people wait a month, or a lifetime, to settle a grudge over a stolen can of gasoline or a wounded dog.

The passing decades stitched power lines across the ridges and laid asphalt roads through the bottomland, where the acres are dotted with white farmhouses, fat cows and round hay bales. Every hollow seems to have a little wooden house built snug against walls of rock and trees. But there are still long stretches here where the thin roads seem merely temporary, a playground for the sleek does that bound light as air from ditch to ditch and the arrogant beavers and fat groundhogs that waddle across the blacktop like they own it, then crash off into the weeds with the grace of bowling balls.

At night, the trees and the up-and-down landscape drape black curtains over the hollows and make the houses seem even more isolated than they are. After supper the men stand on the porches with cups of coffee in their hands and joke about haunts and noises in the dark, and it is easy to imagine that the creak of pine limbs in the wind is really the squeak of saddle leather from some long-dead but restless rebel patrol.

Here, they never stopped praying in schools, and eleven-year-old boys who feel the call stand up in front of congregations in the white clapboard churches and order them to drop down hard on wall-to-wall carpet and be saved. People still fast here — as sacrifice, as proof of faith — when a friend or relative is sick or in trouble, and women who go to the hospital for surgery come home to find tables crowded with covered dishes and their laundry washed, pressed and stacked. There is no such thing as babysitting, but people offer to "keep your kids." Almost every driveway has a pickup, and every toolshed has a chain saw.

Without a chain saw, the ice storms — which come almost every year — would maroon the little houses. Men cut for days at a maze of slick, glittering toppled trees to clear a driveway or a mile of road. Snow they can handle, but they hate the ice.

It is a lovely and rugged place, a fairly isolated place, with just 5,873 people in all of Wirt County. About 900 of them live in Palestine, which says, almost proudly, UNINCORPORATED on its sign. If you want a pizza or a slice of six-inch-high chocolate pie, you have to drive another fifteen minutes or so to the county seat of Elizabeth, population 978, to an Italian joint called Giovanni's or a diner called Mom's. It used to be called Mike's, and when they repainted the sign, they just painted over the IKE and kept the original M. It was a perfectly satisfactory M, and no one here likes to be wasteful.

The young people, the ones who have never been far enough away to realize just how little romance there is in a cloverleaf traffic jam, gripe that nothing ever happens in Wirt County, but that is not true. Elizabeth, named for a woman in one of its pioneer families, almost had something historical happen, once. A marker in front of the courthouse proclaims: NEAR HERE, IN

25

1752, CHRISTOPHER GIST PLACED A MARKER FOR THE OHIO CO., WHOSE PLAN TO COLONIZE THE WESTERN LANDS WAS HALTED BY THE FRENCH AND INDIAN WAR.

Now it has a new historical marker: ELIZABETH. HOME OF FORMER P.O.W. JESSICA LYNCH. There is a marker just like it in Palestine, which proclaims that it, also, is home to former P.O.W. Jessica Lynch. (To make sure, the hamlet of Palestine moved the limits of its unincorporated area about four miles to include the Lynch home on Mayberry Run Road.)

There is no squabble, no tug-of-war. All this is home. The young people, like Jessica, also grumble that it is a place of little if any change. But it is not, in fact, frozen in time. Her house is only about thirty minutes from the nearest McDonald's, less than an hour from the closest mall. And now, when her granddad, the white-bearded Carl Junior Lynch, rides up in her yard, he is on a four-wheel all-terrain vehicle, not his saddle horse. He climbs off, coughs from lungs scarred by breathing in clay dust at a porcelain plant and announces that he has just "got my mornin' exercise."

It is still better than anyplace Greg Lynch, Jessi's daddy, has seen through the windshield of his Kenworth diesel. He stands on his wraparound porch some evenings and wonders why anyone would ever leave — at least for very long. A wrestler back in high school, he is a short, strong-looking man with big arms, a beard and a thick pelt of hair on his body. He likes to fry potatoes in the early morning barefoot and bare-chested, looking a little like a small bear with a skillet in its paw. A truck driver now, at forty-three, he has worked construction, pounded nails, cut hay, cut firewood, hauled timber, hauled concrete, run a bull-dozer, run a backhoe, cleaned houses and dug graves. "You spend four or five hours in a grave," he said, "you know you done somethin'."

What he knows about work he learned by doing it, and what he knows about life he learned, largely, from his grandfather Carl I. Lynch. Carl I. plowed a field hooked to a knot-head mule, did factory jobs, worked for the railroad and was the janitor at the courthouse. He lived, with dignity, to be ninety-three.

Carl I. believed that a man should not be cruel to things weaker than himself, even the lowly serpent. It was Carl I. who told Greg that a blacksnake will run you to death if you tease it, and if the blacksnake didn't get even, then Carl I. would. "If you gonna do harm to it, kill it, don't tease it," the old man used to say. That amounts to torture, he said, and only low men, the lowest, tormented the weaker things in their control. If Carl I. caught Greg or one of the other boys tormenting a snake with a stick or abusing a dog, he would knock them cross-eyed.

That may be why Greg laughed so hard the day his grandpa let his mule's reins slip from around his waist and coil at his feet, causing him to panic, and the faster he and the mule ran, the more the reins whipped at his legs, and it seemed like they ran a mile before the old man figured out that he was not in the coils of the serpent. "I knew it had me," Carl I. said. A star dropped from the firmament, his grandson believes, the day that old man died.

Some lessons from his elders did not take — especially the one about turning the other cheek. When Greg was a young man, three sorry individuals had taken to stealing gas from his car, siphoning it from the tank in the dead of night. He let it go on awhile, letting his anger build, then lay in wait for them one night with a .410 shotgun. He waited till they had filled their can and were skulking away, then he rose up and fired — at the can. An orange fireball lit the trail.

"I asked one of the state cops if anyone had gone to the hospital," he said. "The cop said, 'Why? What'd you do?' "

A few years ago, someone shot his dog, Cody, and left him to die in the woods. It took the dog three days to drag himself home. "I'd always said I'd never spend money on any dog," he said. It was not that he was coldhearted, only that medical help for a dog — a simple pet — was a luxury that his family could seldom afford.

He spent six hundred dollars to save the dog.

"Shit," he said.

Now Cody mostly sprawls in the sun, playing dead — or just sleeping, it is hard to tell. The shooting rests in Greg's mind like a splinter. One day, the shooter will mess up, he believes, and tell someone. "Then I'll get my revenge," he said, "and six hundred dollars won't near do it."

Friends and kin say that he is a good man, but hardheaded, hard to please — if you work with him, it gets done his way. They also say it is a bad idea to make him mad. But he is generous and loyal to his close friends, willing to drive for hours to rescue a friend in a broken-down truck.

Like most men here, he can talk for hours about what makes an engine run, how a

Dodge is better or worse than a Chevy or a Ford, how no guardrail on the entire highway system of West Virginia will stop an eighteen-wheel diesel from crashing to its doom if it ever hits one, even going slow. He hunts deer but almost never pulls the trigger, because that would upset the peace of the woods, which is why he goes hunting in the first place. He likes to watch *Walker, Texas Ranger*, if he has the time, but he and Dee spend most of their time just talking to each other and their children in the kitchen, the center of their life. It has a refrigerator groaning with food, a sleek black microwave that no one has quite figured out yet and a secret candy drawer stuffed full of Twix and Snickers bars, Oreos and Reese's Peanut Butter Cups. It is the worst-kept secret in Wirt County.

A small, blond woman, Dee thought she might die, like she just might forget to breathe, when her daughter was missing. Now talking about the past and about how her family came to be makes her smile. It is like, since getting her baby back, she has learned to taste food again.

A city girl from Parkersburg, she refuses to say that she lives in a holler — it is a "hollow." She works at home for a photography business, on the computer. But most of her life has been here, in the trees, and she is as much a part of it as her husband is.

Greg met Deadra when they were children, when Dee moved to their hollow from town, from Parkersburg, the closest midsize city. Her father had cancer and was dying. They came to the country, thinking it might ease him. She was nine. Greg was eleven.

"I looked at him with his little ol' bald head — his momma had shaved it — and I noticed the top of his head was sunburned," remembers Dee. "I said, 'I'm gonna marry you.'"

"I was on his heels," she said of her courtship of Greg. "I'd steal his toy cars and his army men, and bring them to my house so he would have to come and see me." Over the years, she wore him down. When they were teenagers, they went on their first date — to see *Death Race 2000* and *Macon County Line* at the Sundowner Drive-in. Both were rated R.

"He kept covering my eyes," said Dee. "He said, 'I told your momma I wouldn't let you see a dirty movie.'"

To repent, they drove to church in a cattle truck.

After she graduated from high school, he proposed. Casey Steinspring, a Methodist man of God, married them in his living room in Elizabeth. A little dog yapped the whole time.

They honeymooned at Greg's sister's apartment in Parkersburg. Dee went to work in a sweater factory, and Greg went to work for a chemical company, cleaning up spills. They moved into a home with no running water and no bathroom, heated by a wood heater — it had come apart from heat and age, and they had to be careful when they fed wood into it, because hot embers would fall out of a big hole in the back onto the wooden floor and could have burned down the house. She remembers waking up one morning to pour water from a jug and it had frozen solid, remembers how ice would glaze the insides of the windowpanes on the coldest nights.

Paycheck by paycheck, life got warmer.

Greg Jr. came in 1982. He was a squirmer. He talked, tugged, wailed and screamed.

"That boy was hyper," Dee said.

Janice Smith, her cousin, is blunt. "We should have drowned that boy when he was a child," she said.

She did not smile.

On one early visit to a doctor's office in Parkersburg, Greg Jr. climbed on a couch, grabbed hold of a picture's frame and swung from it like a monkey on a trapeze. The doctor suggested they should beat him.

They hoped the next one would be a girl.

"I had her name picked out my eleventh-grade year in high school," said Dee, who had dreamed even then about what her daughter would look like.

"Jessica Dawn."

She was born April 26, 1983, with red hair and no discernable fingernails. Jessica weighed six pounds, five ounces, and was nineteen inches long. "She was so tiny. So beautiful," her momma said. "The older Jessi got, the more the red went away, and finally her head was covered in these blond ringlets."

She was the opposite of the hyperactive Greg Jr. "She always slept. She was never any trouble. People say children ain't perfect. Well . . . She was always calm, subdued. Even as a little girl, Jessi thought things out. She did touch a hot pot handle once, but she looked at it for a minute first."

Almost from the time she was able to walk, she had an idea of how she should look — not so much out of vanity as a sense of order, of coordination.

Brandi came in 1984. Dee will never forget the day she went to the dentist and left Brandi, then just a baby, and Jessi, a toddler, in Greg's care. It was in the middle of summer, and she dressed the children in shorts and frilly tops before she left. But Brandi had a badly upset stomach, and, as fast as Greg could change her, she dirtied all the baby clothes he could find. In the end, he had given up on taking her into the house to rediaper her. "It was real warm. I just sprayed her with the hose," he said.

Finally, just before Dee came home, he dressed the baby in the last clothes he could find — a sweater and a pair of snow boots. This offended Jessi.

"When I came home, they were both sitting on the porch, tears running down their faces," Dee said.

Jessi pointed at her sister.

"Look how Daddy dressed the baby," she wailed.

Not everyone thought she was perfect. A distant relative, the formidable Eva "Mamaw" Lowe, thought she was spoiled.

Mamaw Lowe was a legend in the hollow. She had a blue and yellow parakeet named Charlie, whom she had taught to cuss. People would walk in her house and coo at the nice, pretty bird.

"You dirty son of a bitch," Charlie would say.

She thought Greg Jr. had fire and personality, and that Jessi was weak, helpless.

"Keep Greg Jr.," she liked to say, "and drown the balance."

(No one in the Lynch family, as far as anyone knows, has ever actually drowned any children.)

"She just didn't like Jessi," said Dee. "She'd say, 'Let me have that kid. I'll hold her — I'll hold her and beat her.' "

Mamaw Lowe lived to be ninety-two, Greg believes, but Dee thinks she may have been mean enough to last to ninety-three.

But Jessi won people over without even trying. Cute is a currency like anything else.

Her teachers describe her as a doll-like little girl who was almost as quiet as one. She cried her first day or so in Linda Davies's kindergarten class because she missed her mom, and that was about the extent of her misbehavior for the next twelve years.

"Of all the children, she was the tiniest," said Mrs. Davies, who has taught kindergarten for three decades. "She was shy. I would carry her around, as she held on to my hair."

She went to school — all the way through — in Elizabeth. She rode a bus that lumbered up the steep grades and hurtled like a big yellow rock down the slopes. She liked school. She got to dress up every day.

"She was on the prissy side," said Dee. "Her bangs had to be perfect. In third grade, she broke her arm on a sliding board, and the doctor gave her a pink cast. She took the strings out of her sneakers and replaced them with pink strings, so she would match."

But she was not the kind of child who sat inside all day with a tea set and an imaginary friend. As little children, Greg Jr., Jessi and Brandi ran buck wild through the forests. They chased lightning bugs through the dark of their yard, depositing them in a pickle jar after their father poked airholes in the lid with a nail. Then they used them as lanterns to explore the hollow's dark recesses. They played softball in the high grass and the mud using their doll babies for bases. Greg wonders, if he dug into the hillside, how many little plastic remains he would find.

"There's probably ten thousand dollars' worth of doll babies, toy cars and G.I. Joes in that mud."

They rode their grandpa's horses — "We had the boots, the hats, everything," Jessi said — and played cowboys and Indians, cops and robbers. They threw rocks, sometimes at one another. "We never let them throw anything at each other's faces," said Dee. "But they did pretty much everything else." They imagined war, and waged it with plastic pistols and pinecone grenades.

"Out here, you had to imagine," said Brandi. Her mother sits on the side porch some evenings when there is still a little light left in the hollow, and she swears she can see it all over again, see them running, throwing rocks, pretending.

It is what they had, Jessi said, instead of sidewalks, subways, taxicabs.

In other ways, the hollow was more interesting than any city street. When they played hide-and-seek, they did not duck into closets. They hid along the ridge line, in three-hundred-year-old trees, and if you were "it," you walked in despair, always ending the game with "Come out, come out, wherever you are!" in defeat.

Jessi was good at hiding. "When I was real little, I hid under the table," she said. She was so quiet, and people walked all around, calling her name. She liked hiding. The time she hid was peaceful, quiet, private.

It would be the one thing — her ability to hide, sometimes if only within herself — that gave her family hope when she was missing.

When Jessi and Brandi got a little older, they played girls' games. They took string and roped off imaginary rooms from tree to tree, and made Greg Jr. play house — even with dolls.

"He chewed the feet and hands off our Barbies," said Brandi, who graduated in the spring of 2003 from high school. "They just had little nubs."

"I tortured them. They were girls," said Greg Jr., a Specialist E-4 in the army, who as a boy would have laughed if someone had suggested his sister Jessica was a tomboy, that she was tough. "If I hit her in the arm, she'd whine and say, 'That's gonna leave a bruise.' " She seemed more concerned with the bruise than with the pain, as if she knew she would have trouble finding socks to match.

"This is a person who got up at five-thirty a.m. to get ready to catch the school bus at seven a.m.," said Greg Jr. "She primped. She ironed her clothes."

She broke hearts from the beginning, not out of meanness, just because — being in elementary school and all — she liked to keep her options open. "My first boyfriend was David Huber, in second grade," she said. "I don't even know why I liked him."

In sixth grade it was Bryan Smith, and as

the years went by it was someone else, and someone else. "I'd try to say something nice," as she let them go. "I was just trying to find the right guy, and none of those guys were."

Jessica tried out for the cheerleading squad in middle school, mainly because she thought she would look good in the outfits, and made it. But the school decided that year that the girls would cheer in shorts and T-shirts, not the little pleated skirts, and that offended Jessi, her mother said. She would never cheer again.

One high school served the whole county. It had good food in the lunchroom, cooked by women in hairnets who would go home and do the same thing for their husbands, just in smaller pots. It had a principal with an unshakable fear of God and a G.I. haircut, and about 390 students, almost all of them white, Protestant and of old, familiar names.

Their accents are not as thick, not as musical, as their parents' — TV and MTV have homogenized and distorted them — but it still sounds a little odd to hear them singing with their twangs over the thumping bass in their Civics, Camrys and S-10 pickups about cruising the 'hood with their mind on their money and their money on their mind.

"You could hear Jessi coming at the mouth of the hollow," said Dee, her daughter splitting the ditches in her Z24 Cavalier, scaring the groundhogs with Nelly, or Ashanti, or Jennifer Lopez.

Jessi played basketball and softball in high school, and she went at it hard — but she was always perfectly made-up as she did it. Her mom says she might have been better if she had not worried so much about how she looked in her outfits.

She made mostly Bs. "Fairly book-smart," said Brandi.

Jessi disliked math. "I loved to divide," she said, "but I hated the rest of it, the adding, the multiplying, the subtracting." (The army would make her a clerk.)

She seems, at first, oblivious to the people who poke fun at her because of her fashion sense, her preoccupation with matching, with order and neatness. Then, almost with a wink, she says, "I would have done more in high school, but I didn't want to mess up my clothes."

People were surprised when she decided to raise and show a steer at the county fair the same year she entered the pageant. "I was the one who got up early and fed it," said Greg Jr. He smiles at the stories of his sister as a kind of outdoorswoman, just because she was born in the country. "She went in the woods once and pretended that she was hunting. My sister just wanted to be pampered."

She was as good a teenager as she was a child. She never came home in back of a state trooper's car, never stayed out all night. "There wasn't a whole lot here to do," said Greg Jr. "Some of us would go to the Exxon parking lot, drop the tailgates and sit and bullshit till the local law ran us off." Jessica didn't even do that, he said.

She and her friends played rummy at kitchen tables late into the night, and talked about boys and the future, which always seemed to be the same thing.

Her best friend was Jessie Boice, now Jessie Lowe, her teammate. She knew her senior year that she would marry her sweetheart, Jeff.

"At eighteen, she found her guy," said Jessica. "That was good. I'm proud for her."

"She didn't find her guy," said Jessie Boice of Jessica. "Her guy wasn't here."

On graduation day, ninety young men and women on the threshold of their adult lives walked up onstage to get their diplomas at Wirt County High School.

She would be the last person on earth, thought many who knew her, to trade her diploma and her wardrobe for a pair of size 5 combat boots and six years in olive drab.

She wanted more than that. She wanted to go to college — nothing fancy, just a place where she could get a teaching certificate — and find a job teaching kindergarten. With any luck, that ambition would bring her home, keep her home — she never wanted to escape the place forever. But first, she wanted to see what was on the other side of the hollow. "I wanted to go somewhere," she said.

Three

Last Chances, and a Chance at War

Long before Jessi, before the recent explosion of red, white and blue in yards and store-fronts, this was a countryside of flags.

People here will tell you with a kind of grim pride that West Virginia is among the nation's leaders in military service, in killed in action, in medals for valor. There are no forgotten wars here. Its people serve, kill the enemy and come home to remember their own dead heroes in the flag-covered mountain graveyards and the V.F.W., and on parade day gray-haired old men squeeze into musty, immaculate uniforms and march in orthopedic shoes along main streets free of fascism and

43

communism because of them.

People do not protest wars here so much as they quietly defer. Churches still hold blood drives after the shooting starts. Travel north on Interstate 77 from West Virginia's capital of Charleston to the Ohio River and you drive a highway dedicated to veterans of the Korean War — until you cross the state line and the asphalt switches to a memorial for veterans of Vietnam.

But as patriotic as they are, younger people are frank here about the reasons they joined up.

For some, serving their country beat the hell out of serving hamburgers.

For some, seeing the world is a last resort.

The very things that make them so glad to live here — the trees, the deer, the life lived free of the complications and aggravations of town — are possible only because of the sheer distance between their front doors and the security of a steady paycheck. Staff Sergeant James Grady, who runs the U.S. Army Recruiting Station at the Parkersburg Grand Central Mall, makes a lot of trips to Wirt County. The closest good-paying factory work is almost an hour away, and those jobs are becoming harder and harder to get. The army, for some of them, is their last chance. Their mommas and daddies order them to get off the couch and go be a patriot.

"Wirt has a high enlistment rate because of its remoteness," said Sgt. Grady, who went to Palestine to talk with three possible recruits — Greg Jr., Jessi and Brandi Lynch — when Jessi was a senior in high school. "Employment opportunities with any future are limited. Most of the factory work is based on nepotism. Most of the retail is fast food."

Sgt. Grady sat on the porch and talked to them about the money they could earn, the training they would receive and — the thing that seemed to impress Jessica — the places they would see.

To Greg Jr., it sounded like he was selling independence. He grabbed it with both hands.

"It means I don't have to work a part-time job busting my ass so I can make money to see a movie," said Greg Jr., who had spent two semesters studying electrical engineering before money problems caused him to drop out.

Greg Jr., a year older than Jessi when he was recruited, has calmed down a little since he was a toddler swinging on pictures in the doctor's office. He is a good-looking, personable, witty young man who can talk paint off a wall. But geography was against him in the fight for his future, and he knew it.

"What else do you have?" he remembers thinking. "One of the highest unemployment rates is right here."

Starting pay in the army was about a thousand dollars a month.

He signed up.

Jessica's reasons were a little different, Sgt. Grady said.

Like any pretty woman from the hills, any woman with solid Bs and perfect hair, she had options. She could have worked part-time and gone to college, or married, even married money.

"She wasn't content with that," Sgt. Grady said. "She was the kind of soldier I would have wanted. She didn't see it as a last chance. She did it for the adventure. She did it to see the world."

As Jessi enlisted, her friend, Jessie Boice, was exchanging vows. She married Jeff Lowe, her high school boyfriend, two months after graduation. He took a job at a plant in Mineral Wells, and she went to school at Mountain State College. She trained to become a medical assistant, but in 2002 she had baby Dylan and left college to become what she calls a "stay-at-home mom." There is not one ounce of regret in her voice. She found what she was looking for in the bleachers at Wirt County High School, and now she has a beautiful, perfect child. "He is everything in my life now. I like being a mom."

She was just one quarter away from graduation when the baby came, but there is no regret there, either. "I am happy," she said. The baby, screaming for attention, gets it, and there is just happy baby noise as she says good-bye.

"I never would have thought she would do something like that," she said of her best friend.

Ken Heiney, Jessi's high school principal, was a little surprised, too. He had in his mind a tiny, delicate girl who never scowled, never frowned and never raised her voice. "Always a smile, a beautiful smile."

An old boyfriend tried to talk her into staying home. He had a good job tending oil wells, and was making good money. He begged her to turn the army down. He promised to build her a big house, to be good to her forever.

"I thought he was cute — looked like Alan Jackson," said Dee.

"Jessie wouldn't have any of it."

Dee worried, but both she and Greg thought the army was a sensible move for both Greg Jr. and Jessi. There was no cushy retirement fund for either Dee or Greg, no rich college fund for their children. They worked all their lives to make a living in the here and now, meeting their power bills, their car payments, and there was seldom an easy, fat month that allowed them to put money aside for the distant future. If Greg Jr. and Jessica were going to build an easier, better life, they could use the army as their stepladder, and Dee would try and wish the wars away until their enlistment was up, until the gamble was over.

"We just wondered where, in her field pack, she would fit her curling iron," Dee said.

Jessi enlisted on July 20, 2001, and left for basic training two months later, just before two hijacked jetliners crashed into the World Trade Center towers and changed the world forever. Suddenly, the peacetime soldiers' enlistment carried a different risk, as President George W. Bush spoke about a global war on terrorism. But Jessi did not have any particular fear as she prepared to leave home. The fierce bearded and robed figures who spoke of the United States with religious hatred still seemed a long way off.

She was eighteen when she left for basic training, a high school graduate with a barely there scattering of freckles across her nose. She liked to shop, and she liked Dr. Dre, and she painted her toenails fuchsia with little sparkles. She did not mind when people kidded her about her prissiness because it was true, a dead-on assessment of her first eighteen years and a pretty accurate synopsis of all she would likely ever be, unless she went looking for an adventure, for a test.

If she had gone to a local college, worked her way through and graduated, she might well have been the most beloved — and the cutest — kindergarten teacher of her generation in northwest West Virginia. Now, in hindsight, that does not seem so bad.

But then, as she passed through the gates of Fort Jackson, just outside Columbia, South Carolina, she did so with a sense of excitement and apprehension. "Victory Starts Here" was the boot camp's motto. Her test, to prove she was more than just pretty, just nice, more than just that benign smile, was beginning.

Four

Boot

The drill sergeant was tall and skinny, a whip of a man.

"Where are you from, Recruit?" he shouted.

"West Virginia, Drill Sergeant!" she shouted back.

"*West Virginia!*" he screamed, as if she had jabbed him with a fork.

She stood in stunned, wide-eyed silence.

"I hate West Virginia."

She stared into his solar plexus.

"My ex-wife is from West Virginia."

She wanted to hide.

"I hate my ex-wife."

She trembled.

Then he lowered his voice to a cold hiss.

"West Virginia," he said, "is not a place where nice people live."

For a second, even though she knew it was against the rules, she wondered if he was going to strike her. At home, people did not talk this way to one another, except as a preamble to bloodshed. As he berated her, she was careful not to look him in the eyes. "They get real mad if you do that," she said.

But it was just words, words used like a rasp on her, on the other brand-new recruits.

"I don't know what his point was, except to scare the crap out of me," she said.

Her fatigues swallowed her like a big frog. They sagged everywhere, and her cap rode low on her nose. She looked like a child who had sneaked into her daddy's closet and tried on his uniform to play soldier. The drill sergeants towered over her — all but a short Hispanic sergeant who was built like a potbellied stove and screamed like a cat in a sack, right into her ears.

She wanted to believe it was not personal, that it was just a jolting, jarring routine — but at the time it was hard to be rational. She had been warned it would happen. "Their whole purpose was to break you down," she said, "and then rebuild you."

Jessi was a target because she looked weak, small. She does not believe the drill sergeants were malicious, just that they figured she might be a weak link, and they tried to break her. "They thought I was this girlie-girl, and they laughed at me," Jessi said.

But they did not know how seriously Jessi took boot camp. "Before she left, I loaned her a military surplus bulletproof vest that weighed twenty-six pounds," said Wirt County Sheriff Andy Cheuvront. "It's a pretty good thing to do your endurance running with — with an extra twenty-six pounds strapped to your back," he said. Jessi trained with that extra weight, almost a quarter of her body weight. It was like running with a three-year-old on your shoulders.

It was not just the drill sergeants but some of the other recruits, too. In the macho world of the military, Jessi stood out like a lapdog in a pen of pit bulls.

Recruit Marcia Wright of New Orleans, Louisiana, who slept in the bunk next to Jessi's, was no bigger, so small in fact that sergeants, as a joke, once made them sleep together in a one-man pup tent.

But Jessi seemed smaller.

"We were looking at her like, 'When you gonna say something?' " said Wright. "She was quiet until you made her talk."

When Jessi did talk, she talked about her family. She talked about her mom and dad, her sister, and a lot about her brother. She rarely argued with the other recruits, even though arguing was almost sport there. "We all got on each other's nerves," said Wright, because the work and the strain were constant. "She wouldn't fuss. She would just let it go. I thought she was gonna be a wimp, but she wasn't."

Her father and mother knew that she was tougher than she looked, but her brother, Greg Jr., did not think Jessica could stand nine weeks of the abuse, the mud, the heat, the fatigue — or the violence. "I didn't think she could hack it — I'm sorry, I just didn't," he said.

Greg Jr.'s transition into soldier had been easy. He was fleet, quick and capable. He knew how to stalk a deer or shoot one from a tree stand, and he could handle a rifle, shotgun and pistol before he was in middle school. He could hit hard for his size — Lynches tend not to grow very big but are strong, pound for pound — and could talk his way out of anything, including, his parents were certain, a court-martial.

Boot camp was not heaven for him, or anyone. But it was, in some ways, like being a kid with free firecrackers, a place where you were paid to get dirty, brawl, hit other recruits with big, padded sticks, scream like a crazy man and shoot free bullets — the army never ran out of bullets.

He guessed — and guessed right — that her superiors and other soldiers might pick on his sister, and he thought that she would just crumple.

He did not want her to fail. He did not want her to suffer, either.

He and Jessi had gone for their physical exams on the same day in the summer of 2001, and were sworn in on the same day. He left for Fort Knox, for his basic training, and Jessi went to Fort Jackson.

Born so close together, they had never been apart. They were not huggy, mushy siblings. They would have gagged at that. But when they were separated, they wore out phone cards, calling each other. She called him Bubby, his baby name, for "brother," or Poomba, just a silly childhood name that stuck. He put a picture of her in his locker.

"He always had tried to look after me," said Jessi. "I remember when I was a little girl, we heard that there was this bad man on the loose who was cruising through the state in his car, looking for little girls and taking them. When we played outside, we would see or hear a car, and he would pick me up and throw me in the weeds, over this bank, to hide me."

Then he would stand there, his fists ready, eyeballing the car until it had disappeared down the road.

But as they said good-bye in Palestine, Greg Jr. knew that Jessi was getting into a situation from which he could not protect her. There were not weeds high enough for that.

Big, tough boys blinked back tears as the drill sergeants ripped into them, nose to nose. They fumbled around for the answer that the drill sergeant demanded of them, but it was never the right one because there was no right answer. It was just the same drama and same abuse played out over and over again. But later, when the rows of bunks went dark at 9 p.m. sharp, the ex–football players and shop-class brawlers took the abuse to bed with them and — some of them — cried themselves to sleep.

But Jessi was not a weeper. In nine weeks of basic training on the drill field and woods outside Columbia, the sergeants shook her up with all their racket and abuse, but the same calm, subdued nature that her mother had seen in her as a child acted as a kind of insulation on her emotions, in much the same way a rubber skin coats a live electric wire. In nine weeks, they never made her cry.

It was not that she did not feel things; it was just that she was a brooder instead of a screamer, a pouter instead of a weeper. The drill sergeants could leave her embarrassed and angry, but she hid inside herself just as she hid under the table as a girl, so quiet that she disappeared. "What is it that the psychiatrists tell you to do, 'Go to the happy place'? So I went to the happy place." And after a while, as she began the two-mile runs and M16 training and forced marches, as the drill sergeants still railed into her impassive face, she even wanted to smile.

"I knew I could do it," she said of boot camp.

There was no seminal moment, just a creeping realization — as she passed test after test.

"I even liked it."

The goal of basic training is to produce motivated, disciplined and physically fit soldiers through a process called soldierization. Soldierization is a tough process that transforms civilians into soldiers. This is accomplished by totally immersing the soldier in a positive training environment established by an active, involved leadership. The environment sets high but attainable standards, provides positive role models and uses every training opportunity to reinforce basic soldier skills.

— FROM THE U.S. ARMY'S
SEVEN CORE VALUES

It started with a fashion nightmare. A soldier took her sizes and gave her four uniforms.

"Well," she thought, "this is disgusting. At least they match."

Then they tested her eyes. The glasses they gave her, government issue and identical in style to her fatigues and boots, had huge, brown plastic frames and lenses that looked like they had been carved from inch-thick bulletproof Plexiglas.

She looked like a cartoon character, like at any moment Elmer Fudd and Porky Pig would each take her by an arm and they would all do high kicks onstage with a duck and a wascally wabbit.

"They called 'em birth control glasses — and they really were. A method of birth control. Ain't no guy gonna come anywhere near you as long as you are wearing a pair of those glasses."

She did not want to see the world that badly.

"I am a four-eyed, birth control glasses–wearing geek," she thought.

The army allowed her some personal clothing, a one-day supply for weekends and off-duty time.

Under a "What to Bring to Basic Training" list, the army made clear what that meant.

No halter tops or ragged shorts
Three sets of underwear (white)
One pair of white,
    calf-length athletic socks
        (no color bands, designs or logos)
A pair of comfortable shoes
Eyeglasses (no faddish, stylish eyewear)
Eyeglass band (if you wear glasses)
Athletic supporter (males only)

The one puzzling item in the army lexicon was what appeared to be a ban on big hair.

Under "Hairstyles Not Appropriate" are listed "extreme bouffant" and "exotic upsweeps."

"Boy," Jessi thought, "I'm in the big life now."

The day started at 5:30 a.m. By 6 a.m., she was doing sit-ups and push-ups, running a mile, two miles, more. At 7 a.m., the recruits rushed to breakfast, and the last one in line had just seven minutes to eat from the moment the last wad of scrambled eggs was dumped on the tray.

The first two weeks of basic training were spent learning the army's values — things like loyalty, duty, respect, selfless service, honor, integrity and personal courage.

But first, every day, they ran.

"I was so sore," Jessi said.

Her first drill instructor for the physical training looked like someone Hollywood had sent over from its latest war movie. He was massive, muscled and could run for days and days without seeming to draw a labored breath. He looked like the Terminator, and some days he would take the recruits to a steep hill and have them do sit-ups on the incline.

They did push-ups until they thought they would drop, and old-fashioned jumping jacks, and more. Always an athlete, Jessi did the exercises with relative ease. There was no fat on her, and as her wind improved and her muscles limbered and strengthened, she got faster and stronger. She did not change much on the outside — she did not exactly bulk up — but she was proud of what she was able to do. The weak-sister persona faded.

The yelling continued, but she was organized, neat, trim and competent, and she followed orders.

She was a perfect soldier, until the hair-bow incident.

Dark-haired soldiers could only wear dark-shaded hair bows or ties. Light-haired soldiers could only wear light-colored ones. It was in the regulations.

One day a drill sergeant got right in her face, or as close as he could without stooping over, and yelled, "Lynch, you know you're not supposed to have that kind of hair bow!"

Her hair bow was perfect.

"Like I would mess up on a hair bow," she said.

She had to drop and give him ten push-ups.

"I guess I kept them laughing," she said.

In weeks three to five, the recruits concentrated on the M16, grenades, chemical weapons, knife fighting and hand-to-hand combat. They beat one another up with batons, hands, feet and knees.

"She was really tough. She would swing from the ropes," said Marcia Wright.

But when the whistle blew to stop the drill, Jessi almost immediately went back to being the quiet listener. "She was meek," said Wright.

Jessi's combat boots were too small. "Her feet, they got messed up," said Wright. "She had a lot of blisters and stuff." But Jessi just wore them instead of whining. "Near the end, they finally got her some new boots."

She knew that she was learning things that could keep her alive, and she soaked them up. She knew it was serious life-and-death training — she learned how to survive a poison-gas attack by being exposed to noxious gas and putting on her mask and gear, and she threw two live grenades without blowing up herself or anyone on her side. (It is in the list of requirements: "Throw two live grenades — successfully.")

She passed every course. During her last few weeks of training, she marched for miles, set up perimeters and attacked and defended them, and studied tactics and night tactics.

"She proved me wrong," said Greg Jr.

She qualified with her M16, even though, she confessed, "I wasn't good at hitting moving objects." But then she never really believed that an M16 would ever be a tool she would need in her everyday army life. She knew how to care for it and she knew how to load it and fire it, and she knew that she was a soldier and that soldiers fight.

But she did not sign up for the infantry. When she graduated from basic training, she would eventually be assigned to Fort Bliss, in the 507th Maintenance Company, as a supply clerk. She would hold a ledger and clipboard instead of that M16, and keep track of and distribute food, equipment and toilet paper. She would become a part of the unnoticed and almost invisible cadre that supports the army's combat troops.

In the old days, they called it "rear echelon." It is exactly what she planned on that day on the porch with the army recruiter and his brochures.

If war was an elementary school play, she would play a tree.

Greg Jr. completed basic training at about the same time. He was assigned to Fort Campbell, Kentucky, to work on the weapons systems on Black Hawk helicopters.

He found what he was looking for. "I got a brand-new car, I got a bank account," he said. "I got money to spend on college." All he was missing was deployment pay — soldiers made hundreds of dollars more a month if they were deployed.

"If I was deployed I could pay off my car — and serve my country," he said.

Jessi's basic training ended with a ceremony at Fort Jackson that marked her passage from soldier-in-training to soldier. She pledged to put the welfare of the nation, and the army, above her own, and to "face fear, danger and adversity" with courage.

In nine weeks, the soldierization of Jessica Lynch was complete.

Basic training was an incomplete and imperfect science. Some people came out with the same problems they came in with, or even picked up new ones, while others did things they never dreamed they could. Fat people got thin. Thin people got muscles. People terrified of climbing a stepladder climbed walls and towers. People who had never thrown a punch in anger — never drawn blood with fingernails or yanked on a hank of hair — learned to kill with an M16, a knife, a grenade. Some people were remade so completely they did not look the same, sound the same, talk the same. "Greg Jr. really learned to cuss," said his mother, Dee.

But in Palestine, Dee and Greg were proud of their children. They looked sharp in their dress uniforms at graduation, looked dashing in those berets. They put pictures of Jessi and Greg Jr. on the refrigerator, framed in American flags.

Greg Jr. began thinking he might just stay in, maybe even go to flight school and learn to fly. Brandi, a senior in high school, started making plans to enlist.

Jessi saw a little more of the world, in the malls of El Paso.

Five

Lori

Friends for life.

Jessi knew, almost from the time they met, it would be that way.

For life.

Lori Piestewa was a Hopi from Tuba City, Arizona. She was twenty-two years old when they met, a tough, capable, well-trained soldier whose dog tags rested upon a pushover heart. She was short — most of the Hopis are — with hands almost too small for her M16. Her hair was straight, thick and a deep, lustrous brown. "She liked her hair," Jessi said. "It was beautiful hair."

The army put them together, making them roommates in a cramped space in the

65

women's quarters at Fort Bliss in March 2002. If not for that, they might not have become best friends, because the uniform seemed all they had in common. In high school, Jessi's friends had been — at least on the outside — just like her.

Lori was from a place called the Painted Desert. As a little girl, she had sprinkled sacred cornmeal on the desert wind to feed the spirits of her ancestors, and then fallen to her knees in the Catholic church to pray to a Holy Mother that missionaries had carried on mule-back into Arizona centuries before.

What could they possibly talk about?

"Stuff," Jessi said.

They were both soldiers, but even in that they were different.

Although it seemed incongruous that Jessi herself would be a warrior, she was from a nest of them. Even the ones not in a uniform waged wars, like the infamous blood feud between the Hatfields and the McCoys that culminated in the deaths of a dozen people in the Tug Fork area in the 1870s and 1880s, all over, as one story goes, the theft of a hog.

Lori was not from a culture of war, although Native Americans have served under the American flag throughout the nation's history. The Hopi, the Little People of Peace, had lived for the majority of a thousand years on the Black Mesa, praying for harmony as their land and culture were assailed by Spanish conquistadors, Mexican and American missionaries, the United States Cavalry and the Bureau of Indian Affairs.

Lori had grown up praying for that harmony, for peace, but by the time she was a teenager there were precious few jobs on or near the Hopi reservation, one of the poorest places in the nation.

She had entered the services as a marine, but injuries forced her out. The dearth of job opportunities on the Hopi reservation and in the surrounding areas nudged her back into the service, this time with the army.

"A good soldier," Jessi said, but that was what everyone at Fort Bliss said about Piestewa, the woman they just called Pi. In a unit that was not really trained for combat beyond its boot camp basics, Piestewa was a fighter.

To Jessi, who thought her grown-up life was just beginning, it seemed like Lori had already lived a good part of hers.

She was the single mother of two, a round-faced four-year-old boy named

Brandon and a three-year-old beauty named Carla. Her children, who were being kept by their grandma, Percy Piestewa, were her life. The army was what she had instead of a man.

"She didn't need help," Jessi said. "She raised them on soldier's pay. She was strong."

To Jessi, it was as if the children lived in the barracks. Lori talked about them all the time, about the lives she would make for them when she was through with this hitch, when she had a little money saved. "There was not one day, not a day, that I didn't hear their names," Jessi said.

Their grandma brought them to Fort Bliss and they played in the barracks, and Jessi — who could never, ever resist children — let them ride her like a dime-store pony. Brandon was short and pudgy and looked just like his mother, and was always getting into trouble. (He liked to play with his mommy's M16.)

Carla was quiet, shy, a big-eyed, fragile-looking little girl who resembled her grandma Percy and who clung to her mother as if she was afraid that at any minute Lori would disappear forever. Jessi became, by degrees, part of that family, just one more person Lori looked after.

Some people you like because they make you laugh, or you like their smile, or they have a car and can take you places.

Jessi looked at Lori and saw someone she could depend on.

Even though the military is supposed to be the ultimate team, she had learned that decisions are made every day that require the sacrificing of people for objectives, and, in the post–9/11 world, life in uniform was all hoo-rah and bloodlust. Duty, yes, but it was something else, something almost like fever.

Lori would never do that, never sacrifice her.

"Your friends are all you can depend on," Jessi said. "You have to have that one friend."

They called each other "Roomy" — never anything else.

Lori's mother, Percy Piestewa, said Jessi taught her daughter how to be a girl again. Lori had gone straight from high school into a life of strollers, diapers and strained carrots, then — just as quickly — into uniform.

"Life was fun for her when they were together," said Percy. "My Lori had been such a happy child, and [Jessi] and Lori were happy together, even if they were cleaning the barracks. They were inseparable.

"It was good to see them together."

They went to the mall in El Paso and ate at Chili's — always the steak sandwich and chips and salsa. "If we wanted to be elegant we went to the Olive Garden," Jessi said. They ate a few thousand bread sticks. "We talked about guys.

"She was seeing this guy who was good to her. We talked about what would happen, how he would react to her kids, whether they could be a family."

They talked until lights-out.

"She would tell me how much she loved her guy," Jessi said, and they would drift off to sleep like girls at a slumber party — with a 5 a.m. reveille.

The two thousand or so miles between Palestine and Tuba City, the gulf between Catholic and Protestant, the expanse between brown and white, was narrowed to nothing by two short women with an insatiable desire for free bread sticks, unlimited salsa and an occasional late-night run for the border at a drive-through window.

Both were from places where young people who had a hard time making a living in their hometown had, for generations, fallen back on the military. But cut into almost any tent on any maneuver in the stateside army, and you would have found the same dynamic inside. There were no rich kids in the 507th Maintenance Company, no trust-fund babies hefting cartons of toilet paper. Everyone there had that, at least, in common.

Jessi and Lori were friends because they needed each other. Jessi needed that one person who would never leave her behind. Lori needed someone to remind her how much fun the ride could be.

The 507th did not seem to be a launching pad for heroes. Its members did their work and collected their pay and knew, with certainty, that the medals and the glories of soldiering probably would go to others because of the word *maintenance* on the unit's letterhead. Still, they talked about and heard rumors of deployment, sometimes with an uneasy excitement.

The politics of it, the rightness or wrongness of a war with Iraq, did not interest Jessi much then, probably because war still seemed so remote and unreal, and because she could not affect the decision one way or the other.

"I didn't even think about it," she said. "I was young. I just wanted to be happy."

At Fort Bliss, Jessi had settled into her

job, and into the routines that went with it. It was not exciting work. "I was the supply clerk. I ordered stuff, and if it didn't get there, I made the phone calls. I was pretty much the housekeeper of the unit. I even had to dock the people who lost equipment." She was raking in $1,100 a month, more than she needed to keep herself in the manner to which she was accustomed — Wendy's, Taco Bell and so on — and enough to put a little money aside for college, for the future.

The day Jessi got word that she was going to be deployed, there was a little excitement but mostly dread. Word had sizzled through the base. The 507th would join the war on terrorism, to finish the job that George W.'s daddy had started and, this time, kick Saddam's ass for him, correctly.

For months, since the airliner attacks on the World Trade Center and the Pentagon, the television screen had been filled with news clips of enraged, bearded men screaming about killing Americans in a holy war, and now the army was sending her as part of its invading force into that maelstrom of hatred. Her unit began to train, in earnest, with its poison-gas equipment, suits and masks and injections to protect them against toxins that would cause them, if exposed, to die in agony.

She did not want to go. "But it was our job. To do our duty."

Funny how those words always seemed so cavalier on the porch in Palestine, listening to old soldiers talk about war.

Now doing your duty meant that you could die.

The worst of it was that her best friend, the person she leaned on, would not be there. Lori had injured her shoulder and had a medical pass out of deployment, out of harm's way.

But that was never really an option, said Lori's mother.

She knew her daughter would go.

"There was no way she would let Jessi go alone," she said. It was like they really were children again. If one had to go to the dentist, the other would go and sit with her in the waiting room and hold her hand. If it had been Jessi with an out, she still would have gone, too, to be with her friend. "They were children," said Percy. "Inseparable children."

Lori told Jessi she would go with her in this way: "You have to. I have to."

Jessi rejoiced. "I didn't think anything bad would happen."

It was war, but their role in it, both young

women believed, would be safe and small.

Jessi called her old friend Jessie Boice Lowe to say good-bye.

"I told her, 'You be careful,' " Jessie said.

"Don't worry," her old friend replied. "We won't be anywhere near danger."

The 507th mustered in a gymnasium that February for the plane ride to Kuwait. The waxed wooden floor was covered in big green field packs. On every pack leaned an M16, except Lori's.

Her son was playing soldier with it in the bleachers. There was no clip in it, which was a good thing.

Everyone took pictures. Carla, the little girl, was not clear about what was happening, but the boy, Brandon, knew his mother was going away and was not sure when she would come home.

Lori picked him up and sat him in her lap and made him a promise.

"Baby, I'll be back," she said. "I'll be back real soon, and we'll be a family, together."

Six

Ruben

The Third Infantry Division amassed inside Kuwait and waited for orders to roll into southern Iraq. The eighty-two soldiers of the 507th Maintenance Company would lend mechanical support to a Patriot missile battery that was being deployed to give cover for ground troops. The Patriot was designed to shoot down missiles — missiles that, at the time, the American soldiers feared would be filled with poison gas. As the soldiers poured into a vast staging area, the sand vanished under a sprawling tent city called Camp Virginia — perhaps the richest terrorism target in all of the Middle East for just a few weeks in time.

The army command, intent on making its soldiers as battle-ready as possible, shocked them out of their sleep with poison-gas alarms. "Every night it was just screams of 'Gas! Gas!' and then the sound of pounding feet," Jessi said. She and Lori would scramble into masks and protective clothing or run for the missile bunkers that never had enough room for all the soldiers. The ones who could not shove their way inside — in a display of survival of the fittest — just waited, almost helpless, outside, waited for the whistle of a mortar or missile. "You just stand," she said, "and wait to get killed."

The missile never came, but the drills made it impossible to sleep, impossible to rest, and over those tense, bitter days Jessi found herself becoming less tuned in, not more, to what she was expected to do. One night, a sandstorm blew their tent away, and they stumbled around in a brown cloud, bumping into people, until they found their way inside another shelter. After a while she gave up on sleeping. She had especially come to fear something called a "Frog Seven," a chemical weapon the Iraqis were said to be planning to use against the Americans. The frog hopped through her half-sleep, until the siren sounded and she stumbled out of the tent and ran for her life, Lori at her side.

Two things — or two people — made it bearable.

Lori was there, to listen to her fears.

And Sgt. Ruben Contreras, showing the perseverance so prized in American fighting men, somehow managed to pitch his tent right next to Jessica Lynch's. He was in the kind of love that Ajax won't scrape off, the kind of love that makes a grown man doodle a woman's name on his forearm with a pen and say things, his palm cupped tightly around a pay-phone receiver, that would make his buddies question his manhood.

But a tender moment is hard to come by in a season of sandstorms and poison-gas drills, so — like untold soldiers before him — he lived it in his mind. He thought about the first time he saw her, asleep in the bleachers in the gym at Fort Bliss, and how he just stood there for a long time, looking at her face. He thought about how she opened her eyes and how green they were, and how he thought, "I need to meet her," but it took him a week and a half to work up his nerve. He took her to a movie and she fell asleep — it seemed like there was never enough time to sleep in the army — but it was *Scooby-Doo*, so there was not a lot of plot to it.

She thought he was just a flirt, but he persevered then, too, and wore her down at Wendy's over french fries. Before they deployed, he had called his mom, Lisa Letorre, and told her he had found the girl he wanted to spend the rest of his life with. "He said he'd met this girl, this girl named Jessi," said Lisa, "and told me, 'Mom, this is the one.' I reminded him he had other things to worry about."

But she thought to herself, after she hung up the phone, that he had never said that about a girl before.

Ruben had been a wrestler, a running back and a middle-infielder in high school, a playground fistfighter who was raised by his mother until she remarried when he was about twelve. He joined the army to earn college money, to study law enforcement and, someday, become a juvenile probation officer. Like Jessi, he had never met anyone that he thought he could not live without — until her.

"The way I remember it," Jessi said, "I was the one calling him all the time."

The army discouraged such romances. Even though he was not Jessi's sergeant, he was still her superior, so they kept their relationship as low-profile as they could. At Fort Bliss, they could hold hands when they were dressed in civilian clothes, but in uniform they had to keep their distance, even if they were off duty. He had left for Iraq first, and she was sure, with all the melodrama she could muster, that she would never see him again. But then there he was, right there in the sand.

Ruben, who was assigned to the battalion's headquarters battery, watched her from a distance and at night said a prayer to protect her from the snipers and suicide bombers the soldiers feared were just outside their wire. The days dragged into weeks, then a month. Finally, on March 20, 2003, the 507th and other supply-line companies got orders to move out, and they said good-bye. Jessi took his picture. There were as many Instamatics as there were canteens. Then, after he was gone, she climbed into the cab of her own truck, and Lori, Jessi and the rest of the 507th joined the seemingly endless caravan.

But no one was playing soldier now. The drills, the apprehension, had turned the adventure into a wearying, deadly serious ordeal. Jessi shared driving time behind the wheel of her five-ton tractor trailer, hauling the four-hundred-gallon water tanker, which they called the Water Buffalo. It may have been that she was tired — so tired for so long — but with every mile her dread grew. She was never too fond of ghost stories, for the superstition that was as much a part of the mountains as the mist. But it just felt wrong, as if the lumbering trucks were trudging toward the edge of a cliff.

She still had Lori. But Ruben, who had sworn to look after her, was slipping farther and farther away.

Seven

Lost

In a way that had nothing to do with superstition, the fate of the convoy soldiers was preordained. It lay sealed in the pages of a map.

Operation Iraqi Freedom began on March 20, 2003. It was a necessary war, the president said, a war to uncover and destroy Iraq's cache of deadly chemical and biological weapons, to oust the despot Saddam Hussein before he could use the weapons against the free nations of the world. It was a war to free the people of Iraq, the president said, a just war.

Jessi's war was with the gearbox of a water truck, and she fought it hand to hand along a myth of a road — it had vanished in knee-

and waist-deep wallows. The soldiers scanned the blue sky for thin lines of rocket smoke, and eyeballed people who watched silently from the roadsides, afraid that any one of them might take a grenade from their clothes, sprint up alongside the cab and drop it in their laps.

Hundreds of tanker trucks, tractor trailers and Humvees had already pulled out from Camp Virginia when Jessi and the 507th pulled in behind, the tail end of a hundred-mile train of trucks, troops and weapons. The 507th had sixty-four soldiers in thirty-three vehicles, including a thousand-gallon fuel tanker, the four-hundred-gallon water tanker, five-ton trucks that hauled trailers loaded down with supplies and spare parts for the Patriot battery, heavy-duty wreckers used to pull the huge trucks from the sand, and the quicker, more maneuverable Humvees.

The soldiers were armed with M16 assault rifles, a few handheld machine guns and a .50 caliber machine gun mounted on a five-ton truck. Even though they were driving straight into the enemy's backyard, the soldiers of the 507th had not been issued grenades or antitank weapons. In the army's eyes, the 507th was not a combat company. Its soldiers knew how to operate a winch, read requisition forms, run forklifts, give first aid, stack boxes and handle a wrench.

They were under the command of Captain Troy Kent King, a thirty-seven-year-old father of three who joined the army as a dental assistant in 1993. He had never been in combat, either. He had taken over the company just before it was deployed. Jessi did not know him very well. Others said that he was a nice man.

The soldiers there knew there was no such thing as a safe haven so close to war — missiles and artillery hit mess tents, field hospitals and truck drivers, just as American bombs hit children and grandmothers and families at tea. It took courage to stand there, just stand there. Jessi says she was scared, scared to death of dying, but she still climbed into the cab of a five-ton truck and drove it into a war.

Again, the front-porch testimonials of old soldiers in West Virginia echoed in her head.

As a child, it had just been words.

Do your duty.

Serve your country.

So this is what that means.

In a battalion briefing back in Kuwait,

Capt. King had been given a CD-ROM that contained his orders and directions for his convoy's northwesterly trek into Iraq. He was also given a handheld global positioning system and an annotated map of the region.

Sometime between receiving his orders at Camp Virginia on March 20 and the fourth day out, March 23, he highlighted what he believed to be the correct route of his mission on his personal map.

With a private as his driver, King led the little convoy from the passenger seat of a Humvee. He kept in contact with the rest of the caravan with a short-range, one-channel radio.

The Coalition Forces' strategy had seemed simple: Rush troops and equipment to Baghdad along this massive supply line. Capture Baghdad, topple Saddam, and the Iraqi fighters, crushed under the weight of the new cliché called "shock and awe," would leave their uniforms in the street.

The convoy would not invite combat. It would avoid it by skirting places like Nasiriyah, a heavily defended city of 300,000 people, filled with Saddam loyalists, defended with tanks and fortified with berms and bunkers.

Nasiriyah would be hard to take even by

soldiers well armed, trained in combat and backed up by heavy armor.

It is unclear what instructions, if any, Capt. King received in a briefing on the mission. The convoy's commanders seem to have relied, at least in part, on the CD-ROM to educate officers about the details. It is not known how much the captain studied it.

But, in theory, all he had to do to keep his soldiers safe was keep up, and keep to the simple, specific route. Even if everything else failed them, as long as King could see the tailgate of the last truck in the company ahead, and follow it, his company would be fine.

But the 507th was not keeping up.

From the beginning it was a miserable journey, with bad luck that followed the little caravan like a hungry dog. Mile by mile the small convoy just came apart — its unraveling all but ignored by the main party ahead.

The trucks, driven by soldiers who had never navigated in the sand, crawled at about fifteen miles per hour. At times the dust was so thick Jessi could not see the road, and over and over the big wreckers swung out of the convoy to pull a stranded truck out of the sand. The convoy began to spread out, losing definition.

Jessi's truck was one of the slowest and heaviest in line. Hands and feet jerked and stomped foot pedals and gear levers, but the tires would not bite in sand, and tons of weight pushed down, and no matter how much they sweated and cursed, the huge trucks just crawled, as if the cabs were in real time and everything outside was locked in slow motion.

By dark of the first day, March 20, the convoy was still inside Kuwait. The soldiers camped — and slept. They would not sleep again, except for dozing as the convoy rolled, for the next three days. By the third day, March 22, it was a force of zombies, scattered for miles across the desert.

Her truck finally gave out in the desert. The transfer case broke under the strain of too many bad miles. The supply sergeant, Matthew Rose, was in the five-ton truck with her and tried to cheer her up, telling her everything would be fine. But she did not really breathe again until Lori steered over in her Humvee.

"Get in, Roomy."

Piestewa was driving a Humvee with First Sergeant Robert Dowdy of Cleveland, Ohio, in the passenger seat. As Rose hopped into another truck, Jessi, with her pack and rifle, scrambled into the back and felt better immediately. Just being close to Lori calmed Jessi. For days, as the trucks had crept across the desert, they had barely seen each other, and when the dust made a yellow curtain between the vehicles it was easy to wonder if there was anybody else still ahead or behind. There were no late-night chats around the campfire, no sleepy, comfortable meals, no hot coffee. There was just motion, and if Jessi saw Lori flash by in the quicker Humvee there was no time for anything but a glance or a wave. "I knew it would be her who got me," Jessi said. "I knew she wouldn't leave me."

A wrecker hooked to the water tanker and dragged it back into line, further slowing the already creeping caravan.

On March 22, the battalion commanders told King that they could not wait for all the members of the 507th to catch up, and the captain sent half his command ahead with the other companies in the caravan.

King waited for Jessi, Lori and the other stragglers to catch up to him, as the main body of the convoy disappeared. That evening, what was left of the 507th regrouped in the desert, and King, with thirty-two soldiers, eighteen vehicles and orders to catch up to the main body as soon as he could, gave the command to push on. He later steered the column off the road and into the open desert, hoping to make up time.

Instead, the trucks wallowed in rough terrain and made only about a mile an hour overland before finding the highway again. No one thronged to the roadside to cheer the liberating army. There was sometimes a wave or a shout, sometimes just a stare. But so far no warfare, not so much as a thrown rock.

In the trucks and Humvees, the torpid soldiers cleaned their rifles, but the blowing sand fouled them almost as fast as they could wipe them clean. Some of the drivers waited on some kind of break, maybe even a few minutes' rest, to do it right, but there was none. The .50 caliber clogged with sand, becoming about as dangerous as a Civil War cannon on a courthouse lawn.

The last tailgate of the main column had vanished a long time ago. King's radio was useless. He could not raise the battalion commanders for instructions.

Jessi's fear of being left behind was beginning to come true. But it was not as a single soldier, as in her bad dreams. It was she and Lori and half the convoy, the ones with the bad luck to be on the tail end of that massive caravan.

The directions had seemed simple.

After moving overland across the Iraqi border, the convoy would proceed north on Iraq's Highway 8, code-named "Route Blue." At the intersection of Highway 1, called "Route Jackson," the convoy would turn left, avoiding Nasiriyah. The convoy would take Route Jackson until it intersected again with Route Blue, then turn again onto Blue.

Route Blue to Route Jackson to Route Blue.

On his map, Captain King had only highlighted Route Blue — a straight line to Nasiriyah City.

"And we were the first to see the war," Jessi said.

There was a fail-safe in place, or at least it had been. A checkpoint at the crossing of Route Blue and Route Jackson had been manned by soldiers to direct stragglers to the detour, to safety. But by the time the 507th finally got there, it had been abandoned.

The convoy rolled through the intersection.

It was near dawn. The convoy soldiers did

not know what was happening to them, but they knew something was wrong, Jessi said, especially after King came upon a marine unit and asked if Route Blue continued on north. The marines told him that Route Blue did continue north and did not warn the captain of any trouble ahead, Jessi said. "We didn't know where we were, and we didn't know where we were going," she said. "We were lost."

Later, the soldiers saw lights winking ahead.

They were happy. They thought it was the main convoy.

They had caught up. They were safe.

But the closer they got, the clearer it became that something was wrong.

The sun came up on the city of Nasiriyah.

Instead of turning around, King led the soldiers through.

The city was beginning to come to life. One Iraqi soldier at a guard post looked at them and waved. Or perhaps he was beckoning.

King "believed in error that Blue was his assigned route," wrote the army in its report. "A navigational error, caused by combined effects of the operational pace, acute fatigue, isolation and harsh environmental conditions."

In the cabs of the trucks, the soldiers knew only that someone had messed up.

The marines at the city outskirts could have told them to turn back — the marines had to know Nasiriyah would be their death, Jessi said. "How do they let a whole convoy go past? Not one person tried to stop us. They just sat there."

The convoy lumbered all the way through downtown. There was no gunfire, no real sign of hostility. But in the houses and behind the walls, Saddam's soldiers and militia were reaching for their AK-47s and rocket launchers and heading into the morning, into the bounty that had been laid before them.

King finally noticed his mistake.

He turned the convoy around. But a company that had had no luck at all so far did not have any now. As the big, lumbering machines made their slow U-turn, one of the trucks ran out of gas. The convoy stopped, and Jessi, Lori and others piled out of the Humvees and trucks and formed a guard around the truck as another soldier poured gas into it.

Jessi and Lori stood back-to-back, because it just felt safer that way. They joked, or tried to, because they were so scared. As hard as she tries now, Jessi cannot remember what they said. It was something silly, something about not getting shot.

"Our feet kept sinking into this red clay," she said, and she hated that — because she knew that when she had to run she would be slow, and she knew from basic training that it was a lot easier to shoot things that stood still.

She heard the first sergeant give the order to lock and load. Jessi grabbed the slide on the side of her M16, tugged it back and tried to chamber a round.

It jammed. She had cleaned it every day, but the grit had swirled in through the truck's windows all day and clogged it again with grime. She snatched at it, trying to eject the jammed cartridge.

She handed the rifle to the first sergeant, Robert Dowdy, who tried to fix it, but he failed to and just threw it back to her in frustration. She held it like a soldier would, but she might as well have been back on the ridge in Palestine, playing war with pop-guns. They had just crawled back to the Humvee when Jessi heard a single, sharp gunshot, then silence, then the gunfire began to chatter, coming closer.

"We got to get out of here," Dowdy said.

But there was no clean lane to flee through. The bigger trucks, their drivers standing up in their seats to grind their boots onto the gas pedals, could not get above forty miles per hour. One of them bogged down in the roadside sand, another broke down, and running soldiers leapt into the thin cover of other trucks as large-caliber bullets shattered windshields and bored through sheet metal, as dead and dying trucks began to block the road.

One soldier, left behind, was not picked up as the vehicles swerved away.

He was surrounded and shot down.

"They were killing us," Jessi said. "I saw it."

Two soldiers from another unit, their wrecker disabled, crawled into the Humvee with Lori, Jessi and Dowdy. Sergeant George Buggs and Specialist Edward Anguiano, who had become separated from their own unit and had been traveling with the 507th's third group, brought with them a light machine gun. Jessi sat on the transmission hump in the back between the two soldiers, and as the fire rained down she glanced to the rooftops, to the windows, to the cars parked on the street, to the walls and berms and ditches and doorways.

"They were everywhere."

Eight

Taken

They scuttled everywhere, a hundred, two hundred, more. They flowed from the doors and windows and swarmed along the rooftops and into the street, and the AK-47s bucked in their hands as they fired on full-automatic at the slow-moving trucks. The Iraqis, most of them in loose-fitting, soiled civilian clothes, did not seem to aim at all, but to just shoot and scream and shoot. Some did not even try to take cover, and stood in the middle of the road, firing in the rough direction of the men and women who stared back at them from behind the bullet-holed and spider-webbed glass of the truck windshields. The Iraqis greatly outnumbered the Americans, about 250 to 33, and they sprayed bullets at the convoy and waited for the Americans to drive into their own death.

"Chaos," Jessi said. "It was like being in a bad dream. You just want to wake up and have everything back like it was. But you can't wake up. You can't make it just go away." People she had worked with in a warehouse were slumped into their truck seats, motionless, or stumbled into the dirt from the ruined truck cabs as the Iraqis closed in, in triumph.

She saw it in only glimmers and flashes, in postcard-size vignettes, because the Humvee was packed floor-to-roof with soldiers, packs and guns, and it swerved and bumped through roads littered with debris thrown there to slow them down. The dying and dead trucks did not explode in action-movie balls of fire, but just stopped, clogging the roads. Soldiers fought from their open windows.

Jessi remembers dark, bearded faces and words she could not understand, and the clattering sound of the AK-47s, and the deafening crack of the American assault rifles in the cab of the Humvee as Dowdy, Buggs and Anguiano returned fire.

Squeezed between them, her own weapon still useless as anything except a club, Jessi could only watch. "They were on both sides of the street, and we were trapped in the middle, and they were hurtin' us bad," said Jessi. The Iraqis used rocket launchers to cripple the trucks. The grenades exploded against sheet metal or blew up geysers of sand. From somewhere, a mortar opened up, the heavy rounds pounding the road. In places, the Iraqis had dug trenches and built berms, and machine-gun fire from those military positions interlaced with the urban warfare from roadsides and houses.

"I didn't kill nobody," Jessi said. She seemed ashamed. "We left a lot of men behind."

To Jessi and the soldiers of the 507th, it was like trying to run in the rain without getting wet. Where were the happy, liberated people they were supposed to meet, those who would throw flowers, not grenades? Jessi had not bought that line completely, but she had hoped it was true. Like most of the soldiers here, she was young and really wanted to believe that this was about democracy, that they really were wearing white hats. But she knew that there would be civilians, either out of fear of Saddam or a generations-old hatred of the Americans, who would try to kill them, and the unwritten rule of engagement had been "If it looks hostile, shoot it."

Somehow, their Humvee kept moving, even as the other trucks died in the road. "They shot out tires. They shot out windshields," Jessi said, closing her eyes to remember and then snapping them open to escape one more time from a fear that is still hot to the touch. The American soldiers jumped from the cabs of trucks and ran for any cover, dragging the wounded with them when they could.

The trucks' own shortwave radios squawked with frantic calls for help, with barked orders, with frustration and fear, but some drivers had no orders, no instructions. The batteries in their radios were dead. They might have killed more of the enemy — they might have saved more of their own — if they had had more to fight with, but there were no grenades, no rocket launchers to retaliate against the soldiers in the berms and trenches, nothing to blow apart the vise that was squeezing tight upon them. All they had, most of them, was the metal and plastic M16, a weapon infamous over four decades for jamming in the hands of its users. One by one by one, they jammed as the firefight raged on.

And even with her mind full of what was happening, Jessi still had a small piece of it that refused to believe, that kept telling her "We're not supposed to be here. We're supposed to be back-line, no-action. But we took a wrong turn. We took a wrong turn."

She glanced at her friend. Everyone else in the Humvee was yelling. Lori was grim, focused, almost calm.

She handled the steering wheel like she was going to the mall and her kids were screaming in the backseat, a long way from panicked, or at least that was how it looked. She maneuvered past soldiers and militia who were trying to kill them, around the debris and dead vehicles, and somehow every bullet missed or whanged off their Humvee.

Jessi remembers looking at her best friend and thinking how wrong it was that Lori was there, in a place where bullets flew past her head. She swore that she could see it, could see one round fly past her friend's helmet and clean through the Humvee.

"She's not supposed to be here," she remembers thinking. "She's not supposed to be here at all."

She wanted to tell her she was sorry, that she never meant for this to happen, that she didn't believe it ever could, but there was no time. Wedged between Anguiano and Buggs, who were firing from both sides of the Humvee, she hugged herself. She remembers more sound than words, just yells and screams of fear and rage, all punctuated with the never-ending bark of automatic fire. The engine in the Humvee roared and the Iraqis screamed and everything smelled like brimstone.

As the attack burned across the 507th, the convoy split into three groups. The first, which was led by King, had made its U-turn — actually it took two turns, because King missed another turn — and was several hundred yards ahead of the others as it raced through the city. The captain's Humvee, driven by PFC Dale Nance, made it safely out of the ambush, as did the others in the first group: Sergeant Joel Petrik and Specialists Nicholas Peterson, Timothy Johnson and Anthony Pierce. King raced on to locate the marines his convoy had stopped to talk to on the way into the city, for help.

The second group was less fortunate. With ten soldiers in five trucks, most of the second group was flushed from their smoking trucks, which were stalled by the hail of bullets and grenades or just blew up from the pedal-to-the-floorboard retreat.

The second group had the only extra firepower, the .50 caliber, but when Corporal

Damien Luten tried to get the grime-frozen machine gun to work, an Iraqi bullet drilled into his leg. He tried to return fire with his rifle, but it was jammed, too. Staff Sergeant Tarik Jackson was shooting from a Humvee when he was wounded. Sergeant Curtis Campbell fought back with his M16, but his rifle jammed, too, just before he was wounded.

In that second group, two others — Specialist James Grubb and Corporal Francis Carista — were also wounded. But Specialist Jun Zhang, PFC Marc Dubois, PFC Adam Elliott and Chief Warrant Officer Mark Nash were unhurt. By what some soldiers would later attribute to divine intervention, no one in that second group had died.

Behind them, on the road they should never have taken, there was no sign of the third group, of the seventeen soldiers, of the ten vehicles that had been the slowest, the most vulnerable.

King reached the marines. Their M1 Abrams tanks came down on the second group's attackers with cannon and machine-gun fire and saved them, saved everyone in that group. But when they clanked on, looking for the survivors of the third group, all the marines found were ten bullet-riddled vehicles — no survivors, no wounded, no American dead.

The Iraqis had taken them as trophies, the dead and the living.

It had been a matter of speed.

The wreckers — all three of them were in the third group — were still dragging the broken-down water tanker and another, smaller truck. The surprised and sleepy Iraqis who had seen them come through the city were wide-awake and ready when the third group — led by Dowdy — looped back through town, slow as Christmas. Only Piestewa's Humvee, with Jessi wedged in the middle, had any speed, had any chance to get through the gauntlet.

Sergeant Donald R. Walters of Salem, Oregon, the soldier who could not grab on to one of the passing trucks when the attack first started, was dead, perhaps the first soldier to die in combat in the Iraq war. Two other soldiers who had tried to run from their trucks were shot down, shot to death, in the road. Most of them were dead. Some had died fighting, but it is believed that some were shot execution-style, in the head. Chief Warrant Officer Johnny Villareal Mata was dead, and Specialists James Kiehl of Comfort, Texas, and Jamaal Addison of

Roswell, Georgia, and Private Brandon U. Sloan of Bedford Heights, Ohio. Private Ruben Estrella-Soto of El Paso was killed, and PFC Howard Johnson II, of Mobile, Alabama, who was always kidded some about his name. One by one they had been killed or taken, because in the end it all came down to who could keep rolling and who couldn't, and the living who couldn't roll were prisoners of war.

Private Patrick Miller, whose truck died in the road, had jumped from one broken-down truck to another, trying to find a ride home, but nothing would even start. A welder back home in Valley Center, Kansas, he had never fired a shot in anger. He attacked an Iraqi mortar position and killed all the soldiers who manned it — as many as nine — before the Iraqis swarmed around him. But for some reason, he was spared and taken prisoner. Specialists Edgar Hernandez of Mission, Texas, Shoshanna Johnson of El Paso, and Joseph Hudson of Alamogordo, New Mexico, who were all wounded, were taken, too, as was Sergeant James Riley of Pennsauken, New Jersey. All of them fought hard, until they were surrounded or wounded.

The tires shot out from under them, their engines boiling, the trucks had all just ground to a stop in the middle of the hell that they were in, or the soldiers lost control of their trucks and crashed, or they were shot with rifles that had been thrust almost inside their cabs, as their own M16s jammed and left them helpless.

In the Humvee, the soldiers fought back. Buggs and Anguiano also had an M249 automatic weapon, and they fired it into the Iraqi soldiers as Piestewa slalomed her Humvee on and on. But it was not a headlong flight for safety. They could have fled and made it, Jessi believes. But Dowdy was in command of group three, and he tried to herd the trucks through the chaos of the battle, even as they came apart and the soldiers were killed. Once, twice, Piestewa circled around to crippled vehicles so that they could try to give aid or just give orders, but it was hopeless. An Iraqi tank growled into the street, and its gun, like a spear, stabbed through one American truck. It collided with another truck, killing the man inside.

"I heard the first sergeant say, 'Piestewa, speed up,'" Jessi said, and now they were running for it, for their lives.

"Everybody was trying to talk at once, and there was all this yelling, but Lori was quiet. She knew what she was doing. I could hear bullets hitting the other vehicles, and I looked at her and I knew she hadn't given up.

"And we kept going faster and faster, and I thought it might all be all right. But it wasn't going to be all right," because on both sides the enemy was celebrating, dragging soldiers away, ecstatic about this overwhelming victory over the vaunted Americans.

"I just wanted it to be over," Jessi said. It had been about an hour since the battle began in the city of Nasiriyah, maybe a little longer.

In fear and resignation, she could not look at it anymore.

"I lowered my head down to my knees, and I closed my eyes."

Just ahead of them, Iraqi soldiers had used a truck to block the road. An American tractor trailer rumbling just in front of Jessi and Lori's Humvee came under heavy fire, and, swerving to miss the Iraqi truck, ran off the road just in front of them.

In the mass of Iraqi fighters, one of them raised a rocket-propelled grenade launcher to his shoulder and sighted the speeding Humvee. He squeezed the trigger.

Jessi, crouched in the backseat, her arms around her own shoulders, her forehead on her knees, did not feel the round that finally punctured Lori's control and sent the Humvee bouncing off the road, straight at the five-ton tractor trailer.

The last thing she remembered was praying.

"Oh God help us.

"Oh God, get us out of here.

"Oh God, please."

Nine

Damaged

Jessi lost three hours.

She lost them in the snapping bones, in the crash of the Humvee, in the torment her enemies inflicted on her after she was pulled from it. It all left marks on her, and it is those marks that fill in the blanks of what Jessi lived through on the morning of March 23, 2003. But her memory just skipped, like a scratched record, from the last few seconds inside the speeding Humvee to a blurred circle of faces staring down at her in what she slowly began to recognize as a hospital bed. The language she heard told her that she had awakened in a hospital under the control of her enemies, and that meant she was a prisoner of war.

She had been left behind after all.

She remembers the first few minutes of coming to, but this, too, she can tell only if she closes her eyes.

She had tried to move, not run, just move. "I felt like I was chained to the bed," she said, but there was nothing holding her down except the weight of her own ripped, shattered body.

She could not feel her legs, could not move her feet, her toes. In the parts of her body she could feel, there was nothing but pain. It was as if the bones themselves had been sharpened and were stabbing her from the inside.

She tried to move. Nothing.

She thought, dully, what that meant.

"I'm paralyzed."

But that couldn't be right, could it?

Do paralyzed people hurt so much?

It was not just her limbs but her back, her insides, her head. She was too weak to scream, and she was scared, as scared as she had been in the Humvee. She had prayed that she would live through the fight, and she had thought that if she did, her fear would evaporate. But now it was back, hand in hand with the pain, like evil twins.

She tried to focus her eyes, but a blur —

enough to tell people from furniture — was all she could manage.

Were her eyes injured, too?

No, she had just lost her ugly glasses.

She never thought that would make her cry.

From the circle of faces, she heard English. One of the faces leaned in closer.

"Don't hurt me," was the first thing she said.

"I am not going to hurt you," the face said.

She did not believe him.

The rocket-propelled grenade had rocked the Humvee, sending it into a swerve that carried it into the just-stopped tractor trailer with enough force to crush First Sergeant Dowdy, the committed soldier from Cleveland, Ohio. He died, it is believed, on impact. Specialist Anguiano and Sergeant Buggs, who had fought off a small army of Iraqi fighters for what had seemed like forever, were killed, either on impact or soon after by Iraqi soldiers.

Jessi and Lori lay in the wreckage. None of the American soldiers saw what happened to them.

The Humvee crashed sometime after 7 a.m., but Jessi and Lori were not taken to the hospital, a military hospital, until about 10 a.m. The hospital was only steps away — minutes away. Still, three hours passed.

Both Lori and Jessi were unconscious when they were dropped off at the military hospital around 10 a.m. by Iraqi soldiers. Lori had suffered a serious head wound. The Iraqi doctors said that they tried to save her, but that brain surgery in the opening days of the war, as their emergency rooms filled with wounded, was impossible. She died before Jessi came to.

Ten

M.I.A.

They had talked a lot about going to Vegas.

In a dusty camp far ahead, between Nasiriyah and Baghdad, Ruben Contreras thought about Jessi — he always thought about Jessi — and wondered where she was. Sometimes there were whole minutes at a time when he did not think about her, but not lately, not since he had pulled away and left her back in Camp Virginia five days ago.

This war had not gone precisely to script. Supply lines had been attacked, and supply-line soldiers watched the horizon, knowing that they might have to fight their way over the miles. The jets still screamed overhead, the helicopters still throbbed through the night and the might of the American war machine still hovered over the Iraqi desert, the dried-up fields and the little towns where people seemed to cheer and wave one minute and stare sullenly the next.

The newscasters still quoted the administration as saying the war was going well, but the soldiers — while never once believing that they would do anything except roll into Baghdad over Saddam's dead body — knew that they were still vulnerable.

To shut out the worries that pecked at his mind, Ruben transported himself ahead, to home, to some civilian clothes, to supersize takeout, to Jessi and his life ahead with her after the war. He knew if they eloped her dad would kill him and leave him in the trees. "We were gonna go to Las Vegas, to have fun," after they got back from the war. They had talked about Vegas in the way young people do, when they still believe magic is real.

He had thought a lot about marriage. "She's perfect," he remembers thinking. "Perfect, really.

"That was when I saw the 507th roll up" — or, at least, what was left of it.

As the trucks limped in, he felt sick.

"It ain't right. It ain't right."

He went from truck to truck. He saw one

of Jessi's sergeants, and he wanted to grab him, shake him.

He shouted, "How are you here? How are you here, and she's not? You're supposed to take care of her!"

The sergeant just stood there, let it wash over him.

Ruben dropped his head.

"I just walked away."

Then he saw some soldiers crowded around the hood of a Humvee that had been used as a grim bulletin board to list the names of the members of the 507th and whether they were dead, alive or captured. He ran his eyes over the names written in a black marker across the tan metal. First he saw just the letters:

"Pi." Pi, for Piestewa. Then, next to that, "P.O.W."

But someone had drawn a line through it, and written: "K.I.A."

Under that, he found Jessi's name.

"Lynch."

"M.I.A."

"A friend grabbed me, tried to calm me down, but I elbowed him in the chest when he tried to put his arms around me," said Ruben. "She was my world."

He walked to his tent, dry-eyed, angry.

"I lay down and I cried."

Eleven

Time Standing Still

In Palestine, late on the night of March 23, Dee heard the knock on their door, saw the man in uniform, so polite and sad. She snatched at the screen door, almost tearing it from its hinges, and ran away from the house, away from what was being said. Greg, sick to his stomach, hurried after her down the gravel drive, caught her, hugged her and brought her back into the house. "The rest of the night was hell," Greg said. "Pure hell."

Long after the army's messenger had left, they could still hear him. "Your daughter is missing in action. Her whereabouts are unknown. She was last seen . . ."

In the early morning, Brandi saw her

mother sitting on the edge of her bed, wide-awake, silent and perfectly still. "It was like she was there, but she really wasn't there," Brandi said. "It is not something I ever want to see again."

Greg Lynch, the tough, independent man who had never been helpless in his life, could not do a thing to help his wife. "She just went into herself," he said. But now and then she would shriek, and the screen door would bang and he would have to chase her again, out toward the blacktop and into the cold, and drag her back, barefoot and shaking.

The next day, he called Dr. F. G. Powderly, their family doctor, "and I told him we got to have some nerve pills, or something." But Dee calmed as the day warmed up. Greg went looking for her once, afraid he might have to run back out to the road to retrieve her, but found her with a neighbor, Wilma Maze, "sittin' in the sun, cryin' in each other's arms," Greg said.

"Then," he said, "the cousins started comin' in."

Their house took on the look of a wake. It filled with kinfolks and friends, many of whom came up the steps with platters of sandwiches and chicken, pies and cakes. Covered dishes and Tupperware crowded the counters. People patted and hugged one another. "To move, people had to trade places," said Brandi, a pretty young woman with brown hair that glows almost red in the sunlight, who still has a few of the freckles that she earned running through the hollow as a little girl. Her daddy, like all daddies, likes to show off her prom pictures, where she stands next to an uncomfortable-looking big lug of a boy. "Take a wire brush to her," her daddy said, "and she cleans up like a new penny." She is quiet and thoughtful and pragmatic, and as other family members broke down over Jessi's disappearance, Brandi sat, often by herself, and picked apart the possibilities of what had happened to her sister. Brandi did not believe her sister was dead.

The idea could not form in her mind.

"I thought she was hurt, and that was why we had not heard from her," she said. Jessi had told her, too, that she was just a supply clerk, and that supply clerks do not get wounded or killed.

It was not the first lie her sister told her.

"When I was little," Brandi said, "she told me there was a monster living under our porch."

She did not believe in monsters under the porch. Brandi is a matter-of-fact young woman. She thinks she might want to be a psychologist.

But she does believe in monsters.

She learned to.

Now and then, someone would walk by the bedroom where the Lynch girls had slept in bunk beds until the night Jessi left for boot camp, or spot a picture stuck on the refrigerator, and would start to cry. Greg was proud of the house his family had been raised in. He and Dee bought it before they could even afford it, a perfect little white wooden A-frame that, snuggled in against the high walls of hill and trees, looked like something out of "Hansel and Gretel." It was built solid enough, on its foundation of ancient timber, to hold up under any storm, and small enough that his children would never be very far away. He watched them grow up right in front of him. That is the magic of little houses.

He had never wanted to live anywhere else and had never minded the distance to town. But in this crisis, he did feel isolated, cut off from the war on the other side of the world and from anyone who could give him any answers. "Nobody was telling us anything," he said. Cousin Dan Little, who is in the National Guard, worked the phone, trying to find out all he could from the army, but there was nothing much to learn. The 507th had been ambushed, with heavy casualties. Jessi's body had not been found, but the Iraqis took the bodies of their enemies, sometimes, as trophies. They filmed them with a camcorder and sent the tapes off to the Arab television networks.

"All we could do was wait," Greg said. He had heard people say that exact thing all his life, but now he and his family learned what an agony passing time could be.

Brandi was squeezed by people who needed to squeeze someone real bad, but she felt lost in the milling crowd. "I tried reading books. I would read the same line over and over again. I'd read romance novels and there was no romance in it," she said. "It just didn't interest me. I'd watch television and not see it. I was just there."

Dee, in her suffering, passed from hand to hand. "I didn't know what day of the week it was," she said. "It all ran together." She cried all day, until she went to sleep with the help of pills.

She woke up to bleary-eyed friends who had stayed up all night, keeping a vigil for no other reason than to keep it, because going home was unthinkable. Junior Collins, big, black-bearded, usually silent,

117

just hovered near, waiting to do something, anything. Greg Lynch had been kind to him, had gone to get him when a truck wreck left him stranded. Now he wanted to help, even if that meant just feeding the fireplace or going to get milk and bread.

Benny Smith, who had married into the family and can talk as long as there is oxygen, stood on the porch and could not think of a damn thing to say. "She's just a little ol' girl," he said helplessly.

"Yeah," said one of the men, "but she's a country girl." Even in despair, the notion that they were just tougher somehow, here up high, made them feel better.

Greg and Dee had constructed a scene in their minds, a plausible scenario, they believed, that made it possible for Jessi to still be alive. She had somehow gotten away from the ambush, and, perhaps with the help of friendly Iraqis who hated Saddam, she was hiding — but unable to contact the outside.

"I always thought someone would care for her, would give her food," Dee said.

Then Greg and Dee just hoped she had found a hole, a place to crawl into, a place to wait. They saw her sick, weak, thirsty and maybe even injured, but alive. "We thought that she might be with Lori. Lori would take care of her," Dee said.

They watched the television news relentlessly, looking for something, anything, about the war, but all it did was scare them more. "We saw those trucks with the doors blown off, the blood running down the side of a truck, all of it," said Greg.

They watched the news clips in which an Iraqi officer pointed to the bodies of Americans who had been killed, sickening images that seemed to indicate from the wounds that some of the soldiers had been executed. They hated the news clips, but every time such an image flashed by, Dee pressed close to the television, until she could feel the static on her face and hands. She looked for any sign of her daughter, the blond hair, the small body.

She turned away from the screen with hope — but also with guilt, because she was relieved that it was someone else.

Not only was it popular to say with conviction that Jessi was alive, but to suggest otherwise would have been stunning. If some had those thoughts, they kept them to themselves. Greg will admit that, when he first heard Jessi was missing, he thought that she was dead. But he found out he could not stand that, because it meant that all the hope and faith that came pouring in was just talk, just fashion, just something to make him feel better, and he did not want to just feel better.

He wanted his daughter back.

"What do you do?" he said.

He pinned a yellow ribbon on his T-shirt and started to believe.

Dee, too, had all but lost hope in her panic that first night. But as the family and friends closed in around her, she nodded when well-meaning people told her Jessica was alive and thanked them for their prayers and their tinfoil-covered offerings.

Now and then, another thought would tiptoe up to Dee's mind, "the most horrible thought." She would not say it because that would let it in. So she just sat with the people who loved her, holding hands, and talked about what she would do "when" Jessi came to Palestine on her next leave, not "if" she would ever come home again.

"I never gave up hope," she said, and while what she went through is much more complicated than that, that is the truth of it, boiled down.

She started cutting Jessi's horoscope out of the newspaper every day, to find what the stars held for her — and because it made her think about her daughter as someone who had a destiny, still.

At Fort Bragg, Greg Jr. had put a picture of Jessi in his locker. "She's hot," a passing soldier said.

"Yeah, well, live with her for twenty years and you won't think that," Greg Jr. told him.

He was on duty on March 24, the morning after the ambush. He had talked to his mother the night before, after the attack but before she knew that his sister was missing. At about 8 a.m., his father called. "Then I just fell back on the bed, and I bawled my eyes out. She was the beauty queen. This didn't happen to beauty queens."

He went to his company commander and asked if he could go home.

His mother ran to the car as he pulled up in the yard.

"You hate to see your mom cry," he said.

She wrapped both arms around him as hard as she could and clung to him.

"They can't have this one," she thought to herself.

She looked up and saw tears rolling down his face.

"I wanted to be tough," he said.

Dee spoke almost every day with Percy Piestewa, Lori's mom, who was going through a mirror image of the Lynches' torment in Tuba City. She prayed every day to both the Catholic faith and an older faith to protect Lori and Jessi. Before they hung up, they told each other that the girls would be okay.

In the A-frame on Mayberry Run Road, Greg Jr. watched his mom cry herself to sleep. He thought about the miracle that people were asking for, because by now — five days into Jessi's disappearance — that was what many people believed her deliverance would require. He was not sure how he stood on miracles. "I hadn't been to church since I was a kid, since my mom made me go," Greg Jr. said. But for this, "even I prayed."

Greg Sr. spent much of his time being interviewed. He did not like the interviews, and he did not like looking into the camera every day and saying that he was sure Jessica was alive, even as he fought off a creeping doubt. "I wasn't going to let my little girl go down in history as Private First Class

Lynch," said Greg. "She has a face. I wanted them to see it."

He did not sleep. He wolfed down food that had no flavor, and he looked at the telephone and willed it to ring and dreaded its ring, and one day he just fell to the ground.

He was fine, only exhausted — he had passed out.

The uncertainty went into its seventh day, its eighth.

Her family had begun to wear simple metal bracelets that said just JESSICA LYNCH, U.S.A. 03-23-03 IRAQ.

One day, Greg collapsed again — but this time on the couch.

"I was on empty," he said.

He dozed, even in the middle of the crowd.

As he lay there, a man he had never seen before came in and looked down at him.

"I'm sorry for what happened," he said.

Greg just nodded, half-asleep.

The man picked up Greg's wrist. Greg would have jerked back at such a familiarity, but he was too tired to care. The man squeezed another simple silver bracelet onto his arm, next to the one with Jessica's name.

It read PFC JOHN S. STUCKEY, JR., U.S.A., 11 NOVEMBER '67.

"I've been wearing it for years. It's your

turn, now," the man said.

"How long do I wear it?" Greg said.

"You'll know when it's time to give it up," the man said, and left.

He thought he might have dreamed it — things like that happen in dreams.

But the next day the bracelet was still there.

Greg figures the man wanted to give the bracelet to someone who would know how important it was, know it was not just a strip of cheap nickel or copper.

Maybe the man was weary of the sadness it brought every time he looked at it.

"I wore them both," Greg said.

At Mom's Diner in Elizabeth, men who would have kicked your ass if you offered them a ribbon before March 23 wore them on their hats and flew them, with American flags, from the radio antennas of their trucks. Over days of uncertainty, yellow ribbons appeared on mailboxes, school bulletin boards and church marquees. High school girls fasted. Four hundred people lit candles around the courthouse as they prayed for Jessi's safe return. The satellite trucks crawled on the writhing, narrow roads. Flags waved.

Twelve

Wounds

Her medical records show what happened in the three hours missing from Jessi's memory.

Her right arm was shattered between her shoulder and her elbow, and the compound fracture shoved slivers of bone through muscles, nerves and skin, leaving her right hand all but useless. Her spine was fractured in two places, causing nerve damage that left her unable to control her kidneys and bowels. Her right foot was crushed.

Her left leg had broken into pieces above and below the knee, also a compound fracture, and splintered bone had made a mess of the nerves and left her without feeling in that limb. The flesh along the hairline of her forehead was torn in a ragged, four-inch line.

The records also show that she was a victim of anal sexual assault. The records do not tell whether her captors assaulted her almost lifeless, broken body after she was lifted from the wreckage, or if they assaulted her and then broke her bones into splinters until she was almost dead.

Jessi's body armor and her bloody uniform were found in a house near the ambush site, the place that some military intelligence sources said she was taken to be tortured.

But Jessi remembers none of this. When she awoke in the military hospital, it was during treatment, not torture. When she came to, the cruelties were over.

Thirteen

The Enemy?

She wanted to dream.

She was awake for only a few minutes off and on at the military hospital in Nasiriyah. It is hard to tell how long because of the pain. It stretched every second like a rubber band. She had been in shock when she was carried in, and now she slipped in and out of consciousness, convinced that the Iraqi doctors and nurses who hovered over her intended to hurt her worse, not heal her. Over about two hours, they bandaged and sutured her wounds, removed splinters of bone and placed the shattered bigger pieces into rough alignment inside her arm, leg, foot and chest.

She almost died from her wounds, and doctors in three countries later agreed that she would have died, if not for the emergency care that she received in Iraqi hospitals. It might have been different if she had been carried straight from the wreck of the Humvee to the hospital, if she had not endured those three hours of cruelty. But by the time she was finally lifted onto the gurney, she had bled so much that her blood pressure was down to almost nothing. She was almost dead. But when the doctors and nurses reached to touch her she cringed, and she would have fought them if she had been able.

The doctors spoke soothingly to her as they gave her blood and fluids and took X-rays. But her distrust was so strong that, when they asked Jessi if they could reset one of her legs, she said no. She pleaded with them not to do anything more.

"I was scared," she said. "I was just so scared."

Her mind could not absorb the fact that one minute there would be killing and the next the enemy would be trying to save her life. "If they wanted to choke me, all I could do was lie there."

She stared at the ceiling, or at least the blur where the ceiling would have been. It occurred to her that she might die anyway. The doctors had told her that they would not hurt her, but no one had told her that she would live. "They didn't tell me anything at all," she said.

She never thought it was a bad dream.

Even though she was drugged and her mind was frayed, she knew the hard, steel gurney was real, that the hospital crowded with yelling, wounded Iraqi soldiers was real, that she was not going to wake up in a bunk bed at home in Palestine or in the barracks at Fort Bliss. The only way she could escape was to slip back into sleep and dream it.

"I just wanted it to all be back like it was," she said.

As a girl, she could hide all day in a refrigerator box. Maybe she could dream a box, or a Heidi movie, something green and happy with children in it, and disappear until things got better. "When you sleep, you get away," she said.

But what refuge she had found in her three-hour retreat from reality that morning was used up. She did sleep again as a prisoner of war, but seldom for hours at a time, and the box was never quite big enough. She would drift off over and over again, but in a few minutes she would be awake, hurting, her heart pounding. On the gurney, sleep came and went like commercials in the middle of a horror movie.

Confusion ruled in the hospital, in the city. The war had come to the Iraqis much sooner than expected.

First, the 507th Maintenance Company had invaded their city with thirty-three soldiers and, among other things, three tow trucks and a disabled water tanker. Then, the marine tanks had roared into Nasiriyah, shooting up the city, rescuing some of the cornered American soldiers.

Now some of the Iraqis were fleeing, leaving their uniforms in the dust. Others — Jessi does not know how many wounded there were — crowded the hospital. But it was not the wholesale retreat some Americans had predicted. The Iraqis in Nasiriyah would not give their city up for some time. "I'm still in the war," Jessi thought.

Before she drifted off, not fighting it but welcoming it, she tried to look around a little better at the hospital, but all she could do was look from the corners of her eyes. She tried to see more, but the pain in her spine and other injuries made it hard for her to turn her head.

She thought she might see Lori, but she

was glad when she didn't see her there, hurt and bleeding. Lori had gotten away, Jessi believed. Lori was free of this hell, she told herself. But she must have been hurt, hurt badly, to leave Jessi like this.

Then, through the fog and the pain, an ugly thought pushed through.

"What if she thinks I'm dead?" Jessi wondered. "What if she left me because she thought I was dead."

It was just the first of countless scenes that played through her head about Lori.

Lori's body had been taken away, out of sight.

But Jessi was right.

Lori was free of Nasiriyah.

Later, Lori's body was carried to Saddam Hussein General Hospital, the civilian hospital in Nasiriyah, although the reasons are unclear. Saddam's information minister already had hard-hitting video images of the American dead, and the living.

That same day, March 23, the Al-Jazeera television network ran close-up video images of American dead, believed to have been from the third group of the 507th. Two soldiers appeared to have bullet holes in their foreheads.

More cameras recorded four prisoners of war, disoriented, wounded and weary. It was designed to send a message: *This is what awaits you in Iraq.*

That afternoon, the Iraqis loaded Jessi into an ambulance and drove her away from the military hospital. The door opened on the Saddam Hussein General Hospital, the public hospital, a place that would be awash in blood from early bombings, where children screamed and doctors treated wounded in the packed hallways. After doctors stabilized her, she was given her own room and an armed guard, an Iraqi intelligence agent, who took up station outside her door. Doctors said that when she got there she was in shock.

Later, the most famous patient of the war lay under a sheet, three of her limbs in bandages, and cried. It was not so much the pain but the feeling, the desolation, of being alone and helpless. She had never been alone. She had slept within reach of her baby sister. She was from a family where her mother would pull one of her teenage daughters into her lap and hold her just because it felt nice. Even after she left home there had been Lori and Ruben.

She knew that her family would miss her,

that they would be worried. But she would have been amazed at what was happening in the place where she grew up, where it seemed that no one could drink a cup of coffee, eat a piece of pie or pump a tank of gas without talking about her, and wondering if she was alive or dead. But in her stark room, "I didn't have nobody." That night, a nurse, an older woman, came to the room and sang her a lullaby, and even though Jessi did not know what the words meant or what it was for, the woman's voice was warm and soothing and loving, and it calmed her, for a while.

"On the first day, I did not believe she would live," said Furat Hussein, one of her nurses. "But God spared her."

She does not know why the soldiers did not kill her or why the doctors worked so hard to save her. It may have been something as superficial as her hair. She was a pretty, blond American soldier and would look good on television, if Saddam held on to power long enough to use her as propaganda. And if Saddam didn't hang on, the Americans would take power in their country, and the doctors could show through their treatment of Jessi their kindness, their humanity. Either way, she had value.

As the days dragged by in a misery of pain and dull fear, she would become more valuable, to both sides, than she could have ever believed.

Abdul Hadi Hanoon was the ambulance driver who carried Jessica Lynch to the civilian hospital. She was unconscious when he dropped her off, then headed back to ferry the American dead from the military hospital to Saddam General.

"I received her from the military hospital where she didn't receive good treatment. She got special treatment in our hospital. We operated on her and placed her in the intensive care section.

"There were ten American bodies as well as Jessica. We buried them. I buried them myself."

He said the doctors worked to save Jessi out of simple kindness and decency. "They were difficult days. Americans were attacking residential neighborhoods and were killing civilians. We were receiving hundreds of patients a day. When we heard an explosion we went there and picked up some dead and burnt bodies. From the damaged houses we were receiving some bodies without heads. The hospital ground was covered in blood. We were only thirty-seven people working as hospital staff, but during all these situations, Jessica did not go without anything."

Dr. Anwar Uday was one of the doctors who treated Jessica.

"She was in shock when she arrived at the hospital," he said. "She was unconscious. We made some quick procedures for her to save her life and provided her with two bottles of blood. We stayed watching her case all night. At five a.m. Jessica woke up and pronounced her first words: 'I want water,' and 'Are these people trying to hurt me?' There were some security people watching Jessica. They were asking us why are we taking care of 'this bitch. You are traitors.' We were exposing ourselves to danger, and we thought that if Saddam won the war that he will punish us. We were trying to explain to them that she is a prisoner, and we have to deal with her carefully."

Fourteen

Hope

On March 24, the day after Jessi went missing, principal Ken Heiney called an assembly at Wirt County High School. Almost four hundred students, teachers and staff filled the bleachers. "A student from this community is listed as M.I.A.," he began. The descendants of soldiers, they knew what it meant. "You could hear a pin drop," Heiney said. "There was no noise, nothing." Then, in a row here, another there, a student began to cry.

Later, students held hands and prayed in the courtyard, at the flagpole. No grief counselors pulled up to the school with pat answers. "Here, in this small community, every teacher is a counselor," said Heiney, who is also a minister. Classes went on that day, that week, but not as usual, he said. "Nothing proceeded as normal from that day." The question consumed them, and their parents, and people who did not know Jessi at all.

At first, it had been almost a sin to ask it.

"Is she alive?" Almost no one said "no." It would have been setting fire to their own faith, like taking their own child's school pictures into the yard and striking a match.

"Look, she could have been ours," said Brady Huffman, who had retired from the power plant across the Ohio River in Middleport. People in the West Virginia mountains and the Ohio Valley and beyond had bound up their doubts in yellow ribbon and wrapped them in flags, and if you asked them if Jessi was still alive, they answered "yes," because in her newspaper photo they saw their own granddaughters and nieces and best friends. Some people would resent it, would despise the fact it took a blonde, green-eyed Miss Congeniality to become the face of war, but it happened — and as the other soldiers in Iraq died with little more than a nice feature in their local news-paper, Jessi's disappearance saturated the mountains and then seeped out and out,

137

into wider America. This war had rammed headfirst into reality — military mistakes had filled body bags. In the wider world it seemed as if Jessi was a chance at more than just a little good news, as if she could be redemption.

But in Wirt County, no one cared much about the politics of it.

"Evening prayer happened every evening," said Wirt County Sheriff Andy Cheuvront. "At the candlelight vigil, they filled up the front lawn of the courthouse and spilled into the street. It was just amazing.

"Soon after the vigil, people kept trying to think of ways to raise money for the family and do benefits and stuff, so they had a 'Dip and Donate' — that's what people call them around here. Usually people donate something to auction off and the people bring, like, a covered dish, and then people that come throw five dollars apiece into the bucket, eat the meal and then sit around and bid. By the time they got done that evening there was over twelve thousand dollars raised. I ain't never seen one bring that much money."

There were other functions, but the Lynch family did not go, said Cheuvront. They were afraid to leave their phone. "No one blamed them for that," he said.

Greg Lynch's press conferences, in his front yard, filled in CNN viewers, and the members of the Methodist Church, on what he had heard — which was never much at all.

"Usually the first words out of their mouths," Cheuvront said of the Lynches, "were hopes and prayers for the other members of her unit, for the other people in the war. They were being singled out front and center, but they kept everyone else in mind."

Every day there were the Lynches on television, gracious, candid. They got a thousand letters a day, said Cheuvront. The family was so overwhelmed, he stored much of the mail in an unused cell in the county jail.

Every night, the florist brought bouquets to the house, well meant, but only adding to the sickbed atmosphere.

Every time Cheuvront got near the Lynches, he walked away feeling more certain that Jessi was alive. "And if you had any doubts they would convince you, by golly. They wouldn't let you doubt."

The Lynch family, in some ways, fooled everyone.

Their doubt was still secret.

Dee even began to cry in private. She and Greg would go for a walk, and she would just sit on the edge of the road and sob.

As the days went by, with no word on Jessi's fate, people in and around her county began to wonder. Some of them began, little by little, to begin to settle for less.

A miracle would have been nice, but . . .

"Everybody had heard about how brutal the Iraqis were to females," said the sheriff. "No one wanted her to go through that, and [everyone] was just hoping and praying that God had spared her, one way or another."

In Mom's, where the locals say that if you leave hungry, it's your own damn fault, the possibility that Jessi had been killed began to take a tentative hold. Helen Burns, who made magic in the kitchen with banana split pies, hated to think that all the hope, prayers and togetherness would end over a grave. But, "well, me and my daughter was talking," she said, "and we said, you know, it just didn't look good."

Others were more desolate.

"I figured she was killed," said Harold Marshall, who made windshields for the DuPont plant before he retired to the town of Vienna. The news channels streamed the stark, pitiful news every hour, it seemed, a soldier's death here, a death there, reduced to words that crawled through a harsh blue streak at the bottom of the screen.

"It happened every day. It was hard to take," said Marshall.

He liked the talk that Jessi was tough — country tough.

But it began to seem hollow.

"I just didn't give much hope to it," he said.

In the A-frame house, the Lynches tried to log all the mail so that, when Jessi came home — when, not if — they would send thank-you notes. But soon they were inundated, and it was then that the sheriff began to store and help screen the letters.

"You had military veterans sending their own medals that they fought for," said Sheriff Cheuvront. "They sent their medals in case the army didn't give her something that they thought she deserved." Some of them came from the families of dead soldiers, from people who believed that the Lynches had joined their circle of grief, or were about to.

And then there was a package from a little girl, who sent Jessi three toys and a note signed in crayon, saying she wanted her to have something to play with when she came home.

In the mountains, day after day, reason battled faith.

Fifteen

Saddam General

The orderly did not say anything as he rolled her down the hall.

Jessi had been hiding again, in her bed, in her dreams, until they found her.

It was not like at home. They found her every time.

She asked the orderly where they were going. He wouldn't answer.

Then he pushed her into the operating room.

At Saddam General, surgeons had continued the treatment begun in the military hospital. They inserted a steel rod to stabilize the bones in her shattered leg and tried to keep her wounds clean of infection. It was delicate work, done even as their emergency room and hallways began to fill with casualties from the American invasion.

There were doctors and nurses in the operating room, waiting for her. Jessi was confused. She had thought they were through, that they had done all they could.

Somewhere close by, a child screamed and screamed, his pain — to her it seemed to be a boy — bouncing off the concrete walls.

Why was she here?

"We are going to have to amputate your leg," one of the doctors said.

They lifted her onto the table.

"No! Don't!" she screamed. "Please. No."

A nurse tried to cover her face with an oxygen mask.

She fought. She whipped her head from side to side, to keep them from clamping the mask down on her nose and mouth. It slipped from her face again and again, and all the time, the unseen child screamed and screamed. Jessi screamed with him as the nurse tried to put her to sleep. Every time she twisted her neck pain exploded in her spine and her pieced-together bones grated inside her limbs, but she fought them anyway.

"Stop," she heard one of the doctors say.

The nurse lifted the mask from her face.

"Don't do it," the doctor said.

The nurse put the mask down and walked away.

The doctors wheeled her gurney back to her room. The child's scream faded as she was rolled away.

She does not know why they stopped.

Maybe, she thinks now, it was pity.

But in her room, she shook and wept, because the doctors had, without malice, taken from her the only place she could hide.

Later, she would hear that the doctors tried to cut off her leg so she could be more easily transported to Baghdad, probably for a propaganda video; that her pieced-together legs would be too cumbersome — and could become infected if Iraqi soldiers tried to transport her by ambulance. She does not know if that is true or not. She just knows she was afraid to sleep, afraid to be awake. Sleep was her friend and her enemy, and she had no place else to go.

She closed her eyes, afraid they would come and get her in the dark and cut off her leg and she would wake in the morning with pieces gone, and that would be real, too.

She would begin to shake when the doctors and nurses walked into her room. Now she knows that they tried to heal her, that they gave their own blood so that she could get the transfusions she needed to stay alive.

The doctors, Anmar Uday, Mahdi Khafaji, and Harrith Hassona, and nurses, Furat Hussein and Khalida Shnan, tried to save her, even at risk to themselves, by telling the Iraqi soldiers that she could not be moved, by trying to find a way to smuggle her out and by giving her attention they could not afford, as errant fire from American tanks and bombs filled their operating rooms with wounded — many of them children who came with missing limbs.

But at the time, and especially after they tried to cut off her leg, they were still the enemy. It might have been different if she could have seen them clearly, if she could have seen their smiles, their faces. But without her glasses she saw only the shapes of men and women, knew that one doctor was tall and thin and one was shorter and stockier, that one of the nurses who treated her was young, and the one who sang to her was old.

Trust came, but in inches.

"I just didn't think I could take being hurt any more," Jessi said.

She listened for the war to drift in through

her hospital window, but at first all she heard was a donkey — or was it a horse? It made her happy for a fleeting instant, just the picture it created in her mind, the sound of hooves, that clip-clop on a hard road. But then it was gone and all she could do was lie there in her bandages, bedsores and rising panic, wondering if, when the Americans finally did come to get her, they would have to dig her out of the ground.

Jessica remembers what happened to her over the nine days she was a patient and captive at Saddam Hospital, but not always when it did. The days fluttered and faded into fathomless nights under harsh lights and in pitch black as the power surged and died, but time was useless to her anyway, except as a measure of fear and pain.

She talks about it in a flat, dull voice, as if the powerful drugs they gave her as an ineffective antidote to her catastrophic injuries still have a grip on her in the white house in Palestine, in her big, high bed covered in plush toys, fuzzy teddy bears and fat, warm comforters. As she talks, it becomes clear that her faith in her survival fluctuated like the Iraqi electricity, from an almost religious certainty she would be saved to a bleak, dread-filled resignation.

"I never gave up faith I would be rescued," she said, but between March 23 and April 1, it would stretch thin and finally begin to break. Like the people at home, she sees it as shameful now to concede that she ever lost hope, as if she somehow betrayed their faith by giving in while people in Wirt County were down on their knees.

All she could do was lie and hurt, and wait for other people to make decisions that would save or kill her, and every time a doctor came near her she did not know if she would be whole again after they put her to sleep and took out their tools.

She could move a little by now. Her spine, fractured low down, around her hips, still short-circuited her bowels and kidneys, and she wondered, day after day, why she had not been able to go to the bathroom. The truth was that there was no way for Jessi's mind to tell her body that it was time — the signal was lost in the damaged nerve like a phone call on a downed power line. But she could shift her weight a little on the bed, could use her unbroken arm a little — any movement caused everything else to throb — could now move her head and neck. Mostly, still, all she could do was lie there.

She believed she was starving.

The Iraqi nurses offered her hospital food, but she was afraid to eat it. Part of it was suspicion — that she would be drugged and then helpless. She would eat only crackers, never more than one or two, because that seemed all her stomach could hold, and juice — usually orange juice. She would drink it only if the doctors or nurses opened it in front of her. "I was so hungry," she said. Her body weight, mostly from dehydration, slipped below a hundred pounds, and kept slipping.

She was afraid Saddam's agents would bang through her door and torture her, or strap her to the gurney, mutilate her and carry her off to Baghdad. But even though Iraqi men she did not believe were doctors came into her room and stared down at her as they spoke to her caregivers, she was never beaten. "No one even slapped me," she said.

She was never interrogated. "No one even asked me anything about our troops. I couldn't answer anyway." Jessi said all she could have told them was that she was a clerk, in charge of pencils, packs and toilet paper.

But her fears of being taken away to Baghdad were real, and when she told one of the doctors she was afraid of Saddam, he seemed frightened and hushed her. "He told me, 'Don't say that name. We don't say that name here in the hospital.' "

As the daylight in her room came and went, the agony in the parts of her body that she could feel seemed to worsen, not lessen, and panic still danced inside her mind every time she opened her eyes. She could feel it killing her. Fear broke down her will piece by piece, and even though the doctors and nurses still treated her every day, she was weaker and weaker and could feel herself sliding away.

Before, she had swung back and forth between hope and hopelessness, on the rise and fall of panic and exhaustion. But she came to a point at which that hope was too hard to sustain, like a suitcase too heavy to carry down a long road.

"I still believed I was going to get home, but yeah, it was starting to vanish."

When she would panic, or when the pain was more than she could take without screaming, an older nurse would come in with talcum powder, dust her shoulders and back, and rub them as she sang to Jessi, trying to calm her. "It was a pretty song," said Jessi. "And I would sleep." She began to ask for her, for that touch, for the songs she could not even understand.

"She told me her name, but I forgot it," Jessi said. "I tried to forget everything."

She believed it would be okay to forget the few good things in order to sweep out all the bad.

There was a window in her room, but she was too weak and broken to go over to it. She began to listen. She remembers the rumble of passing cars. "I could hear a bell ringing," she said.

Then, finally, gunfire.

Close.

She had heard it before, but it had seemed distant, like thunder.

The Americans were not coming.

The Americans were here.

Still, she did not rejoice.

She thought it might be too late.

She slowly, slowly came to accept that the Iraqi doctors were not trying to hurt her from any meanness, that they tried to keep her alive. But there seemed to be only so much they could do. She was still unable to go to the bathroom, and her leg wounds were becoming infected. The spinal fractures were going untreated, and bedsores had begun to eat at her because she could only lie flat or, for a little while, sit up.

One of the doctors told her to try to hang on.

"We're giving you back," he said. "You've got to hang on."

Jessi did not believe him.

"He said they were going to escape me."

But the light would blend into dark with the same scene — Jessi, flat on the bed, all but unmoving even when she was awake, staring straight up, the tears running down the sides of her cheeks.

Every day she wondered about Lori.

"Where is she? Is she worrying about me? Is she wondering where I'm at?" she thought.

She would replay the days at Fort Bliss, the nights they spent at the mall, at the movies. Every day she heard Lori's voice in her head, saw her face in her mind. Lori kept her company in the little hospital room.

Beyond the closed and guarded door of her room, the hospital was being overrun — not by the Americans, but by the civilians caught in the middle of the war. Men, women and children, ripped by bullets and bombs, packed the emergency room and hallways, but Jessi was mostly oblivious to the blood and the chaos. The war had come with an appetite to Nasiriyah.

One day, she believes it was near the end of her time in Saddam General, hospital workers came into her room with another gurney. They loaded her onto it and pushed her into the hall.

"Where are we going?" she asked.

They took her outside.

"Where are we going?" she said, pleading this time.

"I thought they were taking me someplace to kill me," she said.

They wrapped her head in a shawl, to cover her face, and carried her outside to an ambulance. That way, they told her, any Iraqis who stopped them would think she was one of them. Otherwise, in the bloody climate of Nasiriyah, she might be shot.

They told her she was going home.

They closed the door of the ambulance. It was dark inside, and she was still drugged. She should have been happy, excited about going back to her army, but she felt neither. She did not have any faith that she was actually going home.

Even though she doubted that the doctors would hurt her now, she did not know what fate Saddam's henchmen had ordered for her. "I thought they would just drive me out in the desert and shoot me, and leave me there," she said.

But the ambulance driver took her to an American checkpoint, waved at the troops there and was almost killed.

The Americans opened fire. Jessi only heard it, but she felt the ambulance do a hard, fast U-turn.

They had not even gotten close enough to talk.

It was that kind of war in Nasiriyah. Just in the last few days, the Iraqis had fired from the backs of ambulances and from the windows of houses where women and children cowered in the corners. Soldiers in civilian clothes pretended to be friends as they pulled their rifles or grenades from under their robes.

The ambulance raced back to the hospital. The doors opened on Saddam General, again.

"I didn't have a lot of hope left," Jessi said.

The doctors at the hospital carried her back to her room and shut the door, and she lay awake in the dark. The war was close now, it seemed just blocks away, sometimes as if it were right below her window.

She was more than a prisoner of war.
She was a human shield.
The hospital staff worked around the clock to try to save the civilians caught in the cross fire and the Iraqi combatants who poured inside. But the hospital was also

being used as a safe haven for Baath Party officials, and for Saddam Hussein's Fedayeen militia.

The men she had seen in her room, the men she believed were not on the hospital staff, were intelligence agents who had used the hospital basement as their headquarters and the doctors, nurses and patients as a screen.

They knew the United States would not — intentionally — bomb a hospital.

The Americans would certainly not bomb a hospital with a female U.S. soldier lying helpless in her bed.

In the last few days of Jessica's captivity, one of the doctors spotted an American soldier on a nearby rooftop. The nurses slid Jessi's hospital bed over to the window, so it would be in plain sight.

"They wanted them to see me," Jessi said.

She lay there until the sun went down, hoping someone would look.

I couldn't get away. I would wake up and be terrified, then sleep just a little while more, and wake, and sleep and . . . and I knew the day was coming when I was going to die."

She did not believe she would ever be released. As long as the people there lived in terror of Saddam, they would never let her go.

"I just wanted to look up and see a soldier standing there at the foot of my bed," she said.

She scripted it in her mind. She would open her eyes and he would be there, and he would say that he had come to take her home.

Sixteen

A Blonde Captive

The rumor that she was here, a U.S. Army woman held captive somewhere in the city of Nasiriyah, spread through the marine platoons that were already embroiled in one of the bloodiest, most soul-killing firefights since Hue in Vietnam. Some six hundred marines battled what was believed to be seven thousand guerrillas, fighting in weeds and alleys and door-to-door.

Seth Bunke, a six-foot-six, blond recruiting poster of a U.S. Marine, fought a war he could not have imagined at Central Catholic High School in Toledo, Ohio. The marines were pinned down by cross fire on open ground and died in smoking vehicles hit by grenades. A woman taped with plastic explosives ran screaming at them and was shot down. Caught in the open, Bunke was fired on by a man who emptied his magazine at him, the bullets kicking up dust all around him, until there was just a click. Then, with wonder, Bunke killed him. They fired into windows where snipers hid, into cars carrying Iraqi soldiers. "After we shot everybody, we had to go in and clean it up," he said. Inside the cars were dead women and children, used as human shields. He helped dig a grave for a toddler.

"They were lighting us up. It was crazy," he said. In the middle of a dusty street, he and two other marines were attacked by an Iraqi armed with nothing but a knife. "He stands a hundred feet away, and he's running at me, and he's holding this knife." Bunke killed him, too. But there seemed to be no end to them, no limit to the number of guerrillas who were willing to die for Saddam, whom they either loved or feared more than they feared the Americans who had come to free them.

He is the opposite of Jessi, except for the color of his hair. His arms are thick with muscle and his legs look like pulpwood logs. He entered the service to fight, to go to war, and he killed when he got there. But they shared one thing in the last days of the battle for Nasiriyah, a thought a lot of young Americans had. "I thought I was never going to come home," he said. It was already personal, before he and the others learned about Jessi. The story they would hear made Seth Bunke want to kill, and made him proud to.

Rumors had trickled in for days of a female captive in the city, of a soldier with blond hair. Spies for the Americans, and sometimes just gossipers, would hand a sweaty marine a Pepsi and a bit of information. "As the situation developed over time, we began to get some indications . . . that there may be an injured U.S. military member held in this hospital," said U.S. Air Force Major General Victor E. "Jean" Renuart, director of operations. Then, on about March 27 or 28, a lawyer in Nasiriyah approached some marines just outside the downtown area and told them of a blonde captive inside Saddam Hussein General Hospital. He told the marines he had seen her, and she was in great peril. Mohammed Odeh Al Rehaief was in the hospital and had seen one of Saddam's Fedayeen, dressed in all black, slap the young woman across the face.

Jessi said she was never slapped. "Unless they hit me while I was asleep — and why do that?" she said. She said she was never tortured, never threatened while in the hospital. The doctors and nurses would later say the same, that they never saw anyone abuse her, that neither the Fedayeen nor the soldiers mistreated or threatened her.

Jessi drifted in and out of sleep in the hospital, but she never blacked out like she had in the three hours she lost in the firefight. She does not believe she could have lived through more cruelty — especially not a beating.

"What would they do to me that hadn't already been done, except kill me," she said.

Rehaief would later say, in a written statement published in *The Washington Post* and other newspapers around the world, that he came into Jessi's room and told her not to worry, that he was going to get help.

In his statement, Rehaief said a friend had told him about Jessi. He went to the door of the room and peered through a glass panel. He saw "a large man in black looming over a bed that contained a small, bandaged woman with blond hair."

Rehaief said the man was a member of Saddam's Fedayeen. "He appeared to be questioning the woman through a translator. Then I saw him slap her — first with the palm of his hand, then with the back of his hand."

Jessi said she never met Rehaief and does not recall anyone telling her they were bringing help. She dreamed it would happen, but it never did.

But in the streets of Nasiriyah, the story of the young woman in the hands of the brutal Fedayeen took hold in the minds of the young marines, and it mushroomed: She was being tortured, in the most cruel ways, every day, every hour.

"I took it personally," said Bunke. "I took it right to heart. I have a sister. She's nineteen. I thought of Jessi, and I thought of her. I thought of the people who would do that. I wanted to kill them.

"I killed thirty-four of them."

Rehaief's story did not satisfy the military officials, who sent him back to the hospital to gather more information.

The information he would gather — on where she was being held, how best to get to her room and the strength of Saddam's Fedayeen at that hospital — would become useful in the military's plan to rescue Jessica Lynch, military officials would later say. Rehaief had seen the halls filled with heavily armed Fedayeen, he said in his statement to reporters. He said they wore black ninja-type outfits that covered their faces.

There was also a rumor that the high-ranking chemical weapons expert Ali Hassan al-Majid, or "Chemical Ali," was there. He was high on the American military's list of most wanted.

Jessi does not care how it happened. She is only grateful that someone, anyone, told the Americans that she was still there, that she was still alive — that she was sick and weak and hurt so bad, and needed to go home. "I just wanted them to come get me," she said. "I just wanted to go to Ruben and to Lori and to see my family. I just wanted to get home."

For that, she will be forever grateful to Rehaief.

In the hospital, she had begun to joke weakly with the doctors and nurses. She told them she was not eating because she was on a starvation diet — as her body wasted and her cheeks sunk deeper into her face. To combat her bedsores, the doctors took her to a sand-filled mattress on the second floor. Jessi did not like the room because the window was high and small and she could not see a thing from the bed. A curtain blocked her view of the door and the hallway. "I couldn't see much anyway, because of my eyes, but now there was nothing to see," she said. "I might as well have been blind." Her doctors continued to tell her that she was going home soon, that the Americans were close, very close.

The Americans were taking Nasiriyah, as much as they could take any place in a country where the occupation would kill more soldiers than the war itself. In the hospital, the Saddam loyalists were leaving or were already gone. They left uniforms and vehicles behind and blended into the population with all the effort of a change of shoes. Jessi, flat on her back, listening, could only guess at what was going on, but she sensed something was happening. The thud of army boots and the slap of sandals sounded in the halls. Outside the window, the noise of cars and trucks coming and going. By nightfall, April 1, Saddam Hussein General Hospital would be only a hospital again, an understaffed crisis center without reliable power or needed supplies.

In her room, Jessi cringed under her covers as pounding explosions — she thinks they were bombs — went off in the streets around the hospital and shook the walls of her room, and now and then there would be the bark of a rifle. She thought how sad it would be to survive everything, for so long, and then be blown up by her own tanks, her own planes. "I didn't think they knew that I was there. I thought they were just going to blow me up, just blow the whole place up and blow me up with it."

By the night of April 1, all the explosions had stopped, all the gunfire had ceased, as if both sides had called a cease-fire and gone away.

Around midnight on April 1, a small group of Black Hawk helicopters and fearsome gunships came in low over Nasiriyah's dark skyline. Army Rangers and marines moved quietly into place, encircling the hospital's walls. Other marines rolled into Nasiriyah in tanks and personnel carriers in a noisy diversion, to draw attention, to draw fire.

Inside, Jessi lay sleepless, her blood pressure dangerously low, her heart rate high. A man in Jessi's room, she does not know if he was an orderly or a nurse, saw the American helicopters through the small, high window. "Look, look," he said, excited. "Look out the window." From her bed she could not see a thing, but she could hear the *thump,*

thump of the helicopters.

She thought the Iraqis had come for her by air, to take her to Baghdad or to kill her. She felt the panic again, foaming through her like a shaken Coke bottle.

Held down by the weight of her casts, "I just lay there," she said.

From the hallway, she heard her name.

Seventeen

Travels

The preacher's car crunched over the gravel. The Reverend George Hamrick from Gasaway in Braxton County got out and politely asked if he could pray with the Lynches. It happened all the time, and they never said no. He anointed Dee's arm with oil, and prayed for Jessi's safety, and drove away.

The paper came, April 1, April Fools' Day. Dee got the scissors and cut out Jessi's horoscope, like she had every day. She did not really believe in it, any more than she lived her life by the prophecy in a fortune cookie.

"Today is the day you will tell the tale of your travels," it read.

Eighteen

A Soldier, Too

Late on the evening of April 1, American forces had turned out the lights in Nasiriyah. The power cut, the city lit only by the hulks of burning buildings, emergency generators in Saddam Hussein General Hospital hummed to life. The lights flickered on, and the hospital glowed in the surrounding darkness. Miles away from there, the marines rattled through the city in a chest-thumping show of force, trying to draw the Iraqi fighters to them. Above the city, the sleek, black helicopters raced through the dark, toward the glow.

More than two decades before, a mission like this one ended in the Iranian desert, helicopters burning in the sand, rescuers dead.

But this time there was a little luck, and the helicopters settled softly down not far from the hospital.

The landing gear had barely touched down when there was a shout of "Go! Go! Go!" The Special Forces commandos, whose very identities are secret, headed for the hospital door accompanied by, of all things, a night-vision camera.

The commandos, made up of U.S. Army Rangers, Navy SEALS, Marines and Air Force combat controllers, went hard into Saddam Hussein General Hospital. Armed with machine guns, they kicked down doors even as a hospital administrator tried to give them a master key, the doctors would later tell television reporters. The commandos dazed and terrified doctors, nurses and patients with flash grenades thrown into a building that, a few hours before, had doubled as the headquarters for Iraqi soldiers and Saddam's Fedayeen. They screamed, "Get down, get down!" — and the doctors, nurses and patients who could dropped to the floor.

On the perimeter the Rangers and marines took fire, and returned it. But inside Saddam General, there was no resistance — and no one to resist. There were about two hundred patients and a skeleton staff, but no soldiers, no militia. The commandos did not know that, their officers would later say, and they treated their assault on the hospital as if it was still being used as a hiding place for heavily armed Iraqi fighters — to do anything else would have been foolish. Americans had been killed by Iraqis in robes and rags — and this hospital was where that guerrilla campaign had been planned and armed.

The camera, in ghostly detail, captured the tension and drama of the mission as the American military's fiercest fighters moved through the stairwells and hallways, but it did not illustrate the lack of resistance.

The commandos shouted that they wanted to know where to find Jessica Lynch, and one of the doctors told them he would take them there. The doctor led them up to a second-floor hallway. As the commandos moved down the hallway, one of them yelled her name.

"Where is Jessica Lynch? Where is Jessica Lynch?"

Inside her room, Jessi cowered under her covers.

What if it was Saddam's people, come to get her again? It didn't matter that the words were in English; so many Iraqis spoke

English. "Oh, God," Jessi thought, "don't let it be them."

She could not see the door clearly because of the curtain. She lay, her good hand clutching the sheet to her chin, and refused to answer. There was some light in the room, as she remembers, enough to see a man's form as he walked into the room.

And then, just like she had wished it, a soldier was standing there by her bed.

He took off his helmet, so she could see him better.

"Jessica Lynch," he said, "we're United States soldiers and we're here to protect you and take you home."

She did not know what to say, was still too afraid even to think, so she said the first thing that popped into her head.

"I'm an American soldier, too."

She shook as the commandos lifted her up in her sheet.

The first commando gripped her hand.

"I'm hurt," she told them.

She wanted to be able to see them better, see their uniforms, their faces.

"You're safe," said the man who had first called to her. "It's okay. You're safe."

The soldier reached to his shoulder and ripped a patch from his uniform and pressed it into her free hand. "And I held on to that patch and held on to his hand, and I was afraid to let go."

They laid her, gently but quickly, on a stretcher, and carried her down the hall and into the stairwell. There seemed to be no people at all inside the hospital — there were, but they were all on the floor, including the ones who had helped keep her alive.

They passed quickly into the courtyard, and Jessi felt the wind from the rotors wash over her. She heard the hateful sound of gunfire, but it was hard to tell how close because of the noise from the rotors, and then she was being lifted up, into the helicopter.

Someone was still holding her hand.

"Please don't leave me," she said.

The helicopter lifted off, its rotor blades slicing through the dark.

"Okay, this is real. This is real," thought Jessi. "I'm going home."

Jessica on her first birthday, April 26, 1984

Jessica and Greg Jr., Christmas, 1983

Greg, Dee and, from left to right, Greg Jr., Brandi, and Jessica Lynch

Jessica and Brandi, Halloween, 2000

Jessica's Wirt County High School senior photo, 2000

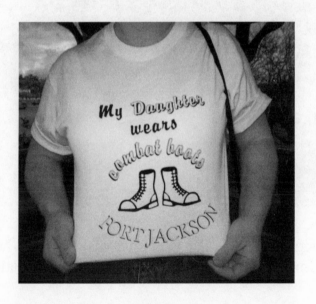

Dee Lynch in a T-shirt commemorating
Jessica's enlistment.

Jessica, in 2000, the year she was crowned Miss
Congeniality at the Wirt County State Fair.

Jessica in her army-issued glasses at basic training.

Lori Piestewa

Jessica, Lori, and Lori's son Brandon in the auditorium at Fort Bliss on the day of their deployment to Kuwait.

Lori, with her children Brandon, 4, and Carla, 3, on the day of deployment.

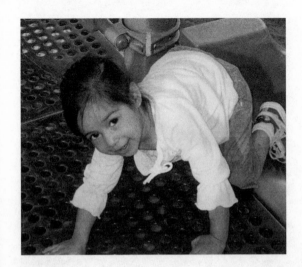

Carla

Brandon

People bow their heads in prayer at a candlelight vigil for PFC Jessica Lynch, missing in Iraq along with eleven other soldiers from the 507th Maintenance Company, Tuesday, March 25, 2003.

Greg Lynch straightens Jessica's graduation photo as Dee Lynch looks through a family album, while they wait for news of their missing daughter on March 27, 2003.
(*AP/Wide World Photos*)

More than seventy friends and family members spontaneously gathered in front of the Lynches' home late on the evening of April 1, 2003, to celebrate the news of Jessica's rescue. (*AP/Wide World Photos*)

Dee, seated center, watches a news report on Wednesday, April 2, as she waits to speak with her daughter by telephone. (*AP/Wide World Photos*)

Jessica is carried on a stretcher off a C-17 military plane at the U.S. air base in Ramstein, Germany, early Thursday, April 3, 2003. (*AP/Wide World Photos*)

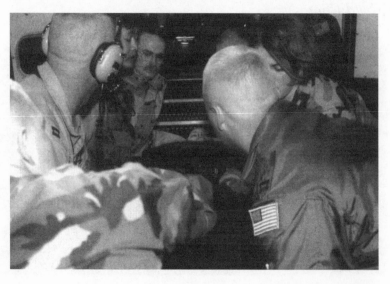

Jessica travels by ambulance on April 3, from Ramstein Air Base to Landstuhl military hospital. (*Polaris*)

Jessica with Sgt. Ruben Contreras at Walter Reed Army Medical Center.

Jessica and Ruben

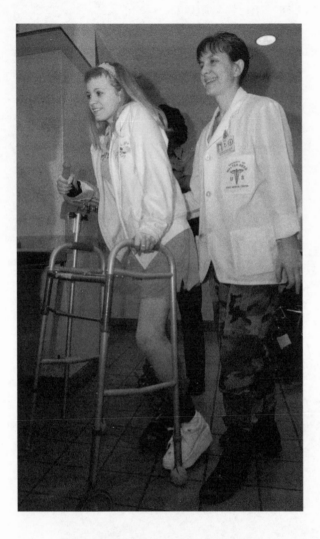

Jessica in physical therapy.
(*Brett McMillan/Walter Reed Army Medical Center*)

Greg Jr. wheels Jessica in to face the media at her homecoming.

Jessica, preparing to deliver her speech.

Nineteen

Under the Sand

.

The mission's primary objective had been accomplished.

"America doesn't leave its heroes behind, it never has, it never will," said Jim Wilkinson, a spokesman for the U.S. forces commander, General Tommy Franks.

But as the helicopter lifted up and away, the commandos fanned out through the hospital grounds, their mission still not complete.

In the hospital basement, the commandos found rifles, ammunition, mortars, maps and other evidence that the civilian hospital had been used to shield the Iraqi military from the American bombers and tanks.

There was also a detailed model of the city of Nasiriyah, built in a sandbox — complete with clearly marked American positions and Iraqi defenses.

Later, one of the hospital staff led the commandos to a patch of sand just outside the hospital. The Americans are buried there, he said. The commandos had not brought shovels. They were killers, door-kickers, not grunts who carried shovels.

They dug with their hands. Racing daylight, when they would be exposed to the Iraqi snipers in a part of the city still not secured, they uncovered seven bodies, all members of the lost convoy. Two more were stored in the hospital morgue.

In the dark, the commandos pulled Lori Piestewa's body from the sand.

Twenty

Miracle

For nine days, work, school, whole lives, were delayed and ignored so that friends and family of the Lynches could be close and absorb a little of the suffering that filled the house. They walked away from their routines, their supper times, their choir practice and *TV Guide*s, just to sit on a couch, lean on a post, and wait. But it had been nine days without word, without even a hopeful rumor, and people began to inch back into routine. "That's giving up," said Wyonema Lynch, Jessica's tiny, white-haired grandmother, who swears she never did. "Lord, though, it was hard."

People who had missed paychecks began

to go back to work. Brandi, who had not been back to high school since Jessi went missing, had to think about grades and makeup tests, and graduation. Benny Smith had put off installing new brake lines on his pickup, and on April 1 he crawled under it with his tools. People still came by, people prayed, and the reporters still interviewed Greg every day and he still told them he knew that Jessica was coming home, but it was by rote now — it had been said so many times that, even though the words came straight from his tortured heart, they had been rubbed thin.

Even the telephone seemed to have a dull, less urgent ring. Once, it had seemed like a lifeline, and every ring had carried a promise or a threat.

The house was full again when it rang at about 6 p.m. on April 1.

Brandi answered it and gave it to her father.

"Someone from the Department of Defense," she told him.

"I thought it was a cruel joke," she said.

Greg took the receiver.

"Who are you?" he demanded. "Who are you? Is this a joke?"

It was April Fools' Day, and they had gotten crank calls before, from twisted people who just wanted to add a little more hurt.

To hear better, Greg took the phone out on the porch. People inside their house, the ones who noticed, wondered if it was important — but it almost never was. It was still a matter of life and death, but the vigil had also become a thing of symbols, of magnetic hope on marquee signs and of flags.

He was on the porch about five minutes, mostly just listening.

He came in and went straight to Dee, still stunned, still not certain of what he had heard, or not completely convinced it was not an elaborate joke.

But he had to believe it.

"They found her. She's alive," he said. She was hurt, badly hurt, Greg told her, but she was alive — and she was free. He said it calmly, but his chest was hammering.

Everything in Dee froze, her heart, her breath, even her mind.

It took a second — a long, empty second.

Then she just screamed, but this time in pure joy. It was a feeling she had never had before, a relief — no, something stronger — that coursed through her body like white lightning.

It was salvation.

Dee had been on the verge of collapse,

mental and physical, for days. She had been hugged and patted by gentle old women and rough-handed, awkward men, but none of it had really penetrated. It had helped, it may have even saved her, but even with her younger daughter in her lap, her son in her arms or her husband at her side, she was still alone with that awful, shameful possibility, and now she shook off all the reaching hands and just ran — again.

She rushed through the living room and snatched at the screen door handle again — "Almost tore it off its hinges again," Greg Jr. said — and she ran, sobbing, laughing.

"They found my baby! They found my baby! They found my baby!"

People just watched her go, as the word went from room to room, around the porch and down the driveway and beyond. "I've never seen my mom move like that," Brandi said.

"She was running back and forth, hysterical. I didn't know what the hell was going on," said Greg Jr. Then he heard the news, "and something just happened in my chest. I came alive again."

The friends and neighbors in the kitchen and the living room began to weep and laugh and steeple their fingers under their chins, their eyes squeezed shut. "Just making a racket and praising God," said Dee, who had finally been corralled by her husband and steered back into the house.

A million questions whirled in her brain about Jessi's wounds — the army colonel who had called had not been specific about what had happened to her daughter — and how Jessi had survived. They had never known she was held captive, only that she was M.I.A. At times she had even prayed that Jessi was a prisoner of war, willing to accept the cruelties the Iraqis were said to inflict on their captives if it meant her daughter was alive.

"What did my baby go through?" she wondered. "What will she be like when I get her home?"

But for now, it was enough to know that Jessi had survived and was back in the hands of her army so that she could get medical help. They knew then that Jessica had almost died at the hands of the enemy, but did not know about the hands of the Iraqi doctors who had cared for her. It would be a complicated story altogether, but for a few hours in a two-bedroom house in Palestine, West Virginia, it was blissfully simple.

She was alive.

All the people in the house jammed into one room — they were coming into the house now every few minutes — and joined hands. "We thanked God and asked that He deliver all the other lost and missing," Dee said.

"Where were the rest of them?" she wondered, the ones who'd vanished from the streets in Nasiriyah.

"Why was she alone?"

The celebration was silenced by that prayer, but only for a moment.

Greg glanced out in the yard.

"It was full of fire trucks," he said.

The word that she had been found spread across the landscape, just as the word of her capture had spread, but faster, much faster. People waved one another down on narrow roads and spread the word car to car, they stabbed at speed dials and squawked on police radios and shouted it in the streets in Elizabeth and Palestine, in parking lots at the Dollar Store and at Giovanni's and over the pumps at the Exxon.

Benny Smith was under his truck, turning a wrench.

"They found Jessi," someone said.

"You're shittin' me," he said.

"Then," he recalled, "a big ol' tear rolled down my cheek."

Harold Villers, the owner of Giovanni's, got a call from a friend. Jessica's alive, the friend said. "Don't you spread any rumors," Villers warned his friend, "until we can find out whether it's true." It took about a half hour for people to hear it, absorb it, then all hell broke loose.

In Elizabeth, people ran into the streets, shouting, whooping, hugging each other, crying in one another's arms. There are never many people in the streets in Elizabeth, but there were then, a place too small for strangers. Fire trucks, sirens wailing, roared down the roads, red lights flashing. Sheriff's cars, blue lights whirling, added their own sirens to the din. Church bells pealed, drivers pounded their horns and within minutes the first of a ragged artillery of fireworks streaked into the sky. People really did dance in the street. It was just happiness, consuming the place like fire.

Big American flags snapped from car windows. Fists pumped the air. "I got my kids, loaded them up and went down to the courthouse," said Debbie Hennen, the Wirt County assessor of property. "I took my boom box."

Lee Greenwood sang "God Bless the U.S.A." a dozen times.

This was no organized function. There was no program. Ministers knelt in front of the courthouse and offered humble prayers as teenage boys hung from truck windows and wahooed. In a country that has honored the dead of the war on terrorism in made-for-TV specials, cable-friendly ceremonies and Super Bowl halftimes, the people of Wirt County celebrated the life of one soldier by hollering, shooting off bottle rockets and laughing out loud.

The television satellite trucks sent their antennas high into the air and broadcast the good news. There had been little of that in this war so far, as the cakewalk many people had hoped for, realistically or not, had morphed into TV images of American soldiers with bullet holes between their eyes and of stricken, exhausted U.S. captives on Al-Jazeera videotapes. Jessica's rescue was, truly, the first good news of the war. And it was celebrated here, in this distinctly American place.

No one remembers a time like it here. And they doubt there ever will be again.

It was the kind of thing that even made deacons act silly. Debbie Hennen spotted Jessi's Future Farmers of America advisor, Ben Cummings, a man who is not prone to hug or get hugged, she said. "I threw my arms around him," she said. "He actually hugged me."

The euphoria spread, in honking cars, all

the way to the interstate exit over in Mineral Wells, where teenagers who had languished in the McDonald's parking lot high-fived one another and then headed to Palestine, because that was where the party was.

It reached the neat neighborhoods of Vienna, near the Ohio River. There, Harold Marshall, the DuPont windshield maker who had feared that Jessi was already dead, saw it on the television. He did not dance or whoop or make a fool of himself.

"I just started to grin," he said.

In Elizabeth, it brought an abrupt close to an administration meeting at Wirt High. "It was perhaps one of the most joyous moments I have had in my life," Principal Ken Heiney said. "We had a prayer, a prayer of thankfulness."

In Palestine, cars clogged the road to the Lynch house. People parked on the side of the road and walked a half mile. The fire trucks that had led the impromptu parade in Elizabeth threaded the needle of parked cars to congregate in the grass in front of the Lynch home, bathing the house in red, whirling light. Cars, people cheering from the windows, formed a parade, and Greg went out to the end of the driveway and just stood there, like the king of England, and waved and waved.

Greg Jr. and Brandi experienced the same stunned disbelief and joy as their mother and father, but as the news became more real, more credible, in their minds, they began to cry and laugh and hug like everyone else. Greg Jr. was still trying to get what he guessed was his heart to feel right again. The most beautiful thing about it all was the look on his mother's face.

He watched her run, heard her almost hysterical laughter, and it made him feel better than he ever believed he could feel. He had always been a momma's boy, the kind of child who called home and, if his father answered the phone, immediately said, "Is Mom there?"

Watching her face and the emptiness in it during Jessi's captivity had made him rage inside — at the people who had taken his sister.

"I couldn't do nothing," he said.

Now he just watched her in the best few minutes he had ever had. "It wouldn't have mattered to me if she had knocked the whole house down, knocked it off its foundation," he said.

Brandi, perhaps the least excitable and most subdued of all the Lynches, still more or less managed to calmly take in everything that was happening around her. "I'm surprised the windows didn't shatter. People came from everywhere — I saw people in our house that night that I had never seen before," people who just wanted to be there. The house swelled with people, and the ones who could not squeeze inside hovered by the open door and the windows, afraid they might miss something. People danced, to no music at all. At 2 a.m., it still raged on, and Brandi had never seen people act that way who were not all liquored up. But they were drunk, drunk with relief, drunk with happiness.

In the early morning, as the celebration rolled on and on in Palestine, Dee began to hear the word *hero*. Jessi was a hero because she survived. They did not know how bravely she had fought, or how she was captured, or what she had endured as a prisoner of war. But she was a hero, friends and family said, because she went there, because she got in a truck and went to war, because people tried to kill her in the desert.

Dee just hugged them. They were all heroes, weren't they, all the young people of the 507th who were in that lost convoy — Jessi, Lori, the rest. Being there was enough, for a medal, for that word. But the truth was, it didn't make one bit of difference to Dee then, and it barely matters now.

When she prayed again, when the crowd finally dispersed and the daylight crept into the house, Dee prayed in unquestioning gratitude to a God of miracles. After a nine-day, unrelenting hell, after praying for God to save her child, her child was saved.

Jessi had given the people of the mountains something that they had never had before. They had always had faith, they had always believed in miracles, and they had prayed for them over their lifetimes. They had never demanded proof, because faith is what you have when there is no proof, no logic, no reason. Faith is what sustained the people here through the crib deaths and highway crashes and cancer wards.

When Jessi disappeared, the whole county asked for God's help, congregation by congregation, house by house. As the days leaked past, people here knew that reason and logic would not deliver Jessi — reason and logic could only bury her. It had taken too long. On the ninth day, Jessi was not going to be found; Jessi had to be brought back from the dead.

"I am a Baptist minister," said Ken Heiney, the high school principal. "I had never seen a miracle, something most of us have never seen. But I have believed in these things, in miracles, all my life."

Then a television camera showed him a wounded soldier on a stretcher, a weak, hurt version of the smiling girl he had often said hello to in the hall.

"We saw a miracle."

She was the validation of their belief, something that they had waited for all their lives. As much as they loved Jessi, or loved the idea of her, part of their celebration was of the proof that she had provided.

"We're not just rejoicing Jessi's life," said Debbie Hennen. "We're rejoicing God's miracle. You know she is chosen — for something that is bigger than all of us. We're convinced that's why she is here today."

It was pronounced a miracle in the governor's office, and over the handlebars of her grandfather's four-wheeler. "God got her out," Carl Junior said. "That's what happened there."

"If she'd been in there a couple more days, she wouldn't have made it out. It was a miracle." He got on his machine and roared off, his comfortable shoes on the footrests, his point made.

Greg Jr. thought a lot about it at the time. The young man who had quit going to church when his momma stopped making him, who tried desperately to find help for his sister in an uncertain prayer in the darkest time of their lives, never pounded a Bible in his life. "They say it's a miracle, but not everybody believes in miracles," he said.

It's just that it is hard to find many people like that here.

"People here gave us hope and prayer," he said.

Was it just tradition, just folklore? Or does he believe in miracles, too?

"I've never seen anybody die. But Jessi was there, with people falling left and right, left and right.

"Knowing what I know," he said, "I do."

Twenty-one

Love Letters

In an army camp in Iraq, Ruben Contreras had trouble keeping his food down.

"I couldn't eat, I couldn't sleep," he said.

The thought hit him — "she might not come back" — and he was sick again. "We heard they were finding bodies," he said.

Then, just like that, his first sergeant walked up and told him that she was alive.

Ruben did what young men do.

He wrote her a love letter, full of promises.

He did not try to be cool or macho.

He poured his heart out, writing as fast as he could.

"When you get back, we'll be together.

We're gonna be all right. You're gonna be all right. If we can make it through this, we can make it through anything." But the letter never quite caught up with Jessi, and when he came back to Fort Bliss weeks later, that letter had wound its way around the world and was waiting for him there, unread.

Twenty-two

"Come Get Me"

The first few seconds of the fuzzy, long-distance phone call still haunt Greg Lynch. In Jessi's voice, he had his first hint that his daughter had been through more than a battle, that she had survived something that could not be covered over with a flag or pinned back together with a medal.

He and Dee waited all day for the call. Even though they knew that Jessi was alive, it still would not be official somehow in their own minds until they heard her voice. It was all they could think about or talk about. "We just needed to hear her, if only for a second, to know that she was not on her deathbed," said Dee.

"Daddy?"

The voice was sleepy, drugged and so weak it broke his heart.

"Jessi? Baby?"

"Daddy, they broke my arm."

It was Jessi's first telephone call home after she was rescued from the hospital in Nasiriyah, and the first and only time that she would hint at what had happened to her in those three hours before she was carried by Iraqi soldiers into the emergency room.

"You'll be all right, baby. You'll get over this."

"The Iraqi man broke my arm."

He wishes sometimes that he had pressed her on what she meant just then, that he had asked her to tell him more, but he was afraid to push, because Jessica sounded so strained, so barely there — and he let the moment, and opportunity, pass.

She would later say she did not remember saying it, and she would never say anything like it again. At the time, Greg knew that she had been broken and mangled, but he did not know about the three missing hours — or the cruelty they had contained.

"I know that they tortured my baby, that they tormented her," Greg said. He guessed it then — what else could the words mean?

But he figured there would be plenty of

time to talk about that meanness in the future, and he did not want to fill this precious time up with that ugliness.

"I just wish I'd thought to ask her more, but . . . but it don't matter. It don't matter," he said.

He believes, like Dee, that Jessi had begun to remember what happened to her and just picked it from her mind like a splinter — along with the rest of it — and that made the hurt disappear. Jessi's psychologists, in more clinical language, would say the same.

The phone call had come in the early evening of April 2 from Landstuhl Regional Medical Center in Germany, where Jessi had been flown just hours after her rescue. At the time, Greg and Dee just wanted to convince themselves, through hearing her voice, that Jessi would live, that she would recover.

"Are you gonna come get me?" she asked.

"Soon."

"My back hurts . . ."

Greg didn't know what to say.

"How will you come?" Jessi asked.

He didn't know what to say about that, either.

"I'm tired . . ."

"I know," Greg said.

"How can you come get me? You're so far away."

Greg said he would have to figure that out.

"We'll be there. We'll be there as soon as we can." The truth was that the Lynches had no idea when they would get to see their daughter, if the army would allow them to see her right away or how they would get there.

He handed the telephone to Dee, his eyes red, his mind whirling.

"Hi, Mommy," Jessi said.

"I had dreamed about that," Dee said later. "I tried so hard not to cry. It was such a relief, but I could just see her there. I could see her in pain."

Jessi spoke only a few minutes. Before she hung up, she told them that she was hungry.

"We just hugged each other and cried, because we knew she was gonna live," Dee said.

She spoke to the doctor that day, and it had scared her to death all over again. It was the first time she had a rundown of Jessi's injuries, and as the doctor went through the litany of Jessi's damage, Dee kept wishing that he would stop, but he just kept going.

Her spine, the doctor told her, would have

to be repaired with metal plates. There was nerve damage.

"Is she gonna be okay?" asked Dee. "Will she walk?"

Gene Bolles, a civilian neurosurgeon, told her he could not say for sure. He said he did not want to give her any false hope, Dee said.

"I thought of Jessi, crawling on the floor with her baby cousins, thought of her so active, and could not imagine her in a wheelchair," Dee said. "But she was alive, and it was all that mattered." She knows people say that because it is the right thing to say. To Dee, as ugly as the thought was that Jessi would be in a chair or on crutches for life, she still would have rejoiced — even if Jessi had come to them unmoving or incomplete.

It was expecting too much, to get her back good as new.

The doctors would have to replace the steel rod the Iraqis had implanted in her shattered leg. "It was from the 1940s," Dee said. "It was too big for her small bones."

The American doctors would applaud the efforts of the Iraqi doctors, saying they did a good job with the little they had to work with, Dee said. But it would become more evident, she said, that the commandos had not only freed Jessica, they had saved her.

The doctors told Dee that the surgeons were still picking splinters of bone from Jessi's wounds, flushing her wounds, fighting infection, fighting a fever that, for someone as weak as Jessi, could be lethal. They also said doctors cleaned two gunshot wounds, Dee said. She flinched at that, because it was the first time she had heard that Jessi had been shot.

At the time, all Dee and Greg knew was that Jessi had been badly hurt somehow in the battle of Nasiriyah. Over the next few days they would hear and read that Jessi had been injured in the crash of the Humvee but that she had crawled from it with her gun blazing, killing the enemy as they closed in around her until she was cut down by Iraqi fire.

Twenty-three

Heroes Everywhere

The hero of Operation Iraqi Freedom went into surgery with a tiny teddy bear tucked beside her cheek.

The myth was made while she was sleeping. Between surgeries on her back, legs, arm and more, Jessi drifted along on the powerful painkillers that dripped into her arm in her room at Landstuhl military hospital.

But as she drifted, as she talked drowsily with her mother and father on the phone, the myth was taking shape in the form of off-the-record interviews with U.S. military officials and overheard snatches of conversation from Iraqi military radio.

When it reached Dee and Greg Lynch in Palestine, it made them proud.

The war needed a hero then, badly. The war's planners needed a clear win, not just unspecific images of bombs dropping and dust exploding, or some mood-catching shot of a young man in desert khaki staring off at the blue horizon.

Even as everyone from the president down warned that this could be a long and painful war, it became clear — as the fighting raged into its second week — that this conflict would be longer, and more costly, than the American public might accept.

This was not Desert Storm, with legions of tanks incinerating the enemy inside his own armor as thousands of uniformed soldiers gratefully surrendered. The U.S. advance on Baghdad seemed bogged down in small, bloody battles, mistakes and underestimation of the enemy's will and ability to fight.

Saddam's Fedayeen did not line up in the desert to be bombed into dust by American planes. They hid in hospitals and homes and covered themselves in women and children in private cars. They killed Iraqi citizens who celebrated the American invasion a little too soon — one woman was killed just for waving at the marines.

The disaster of the 507th was just part of the war's bloody beginning. In firefights in Nasiriyah, eighteen marines were killed. In Kuwait, a sergeant used his M16 and seven grenades to attack and kill two of his officers and wound others, in the first fragging since Vietnam. Television images of children, arms missing, showed the cost of the war to the civilian population of Iraq.

Still, even as protests packed the streets in America and in Great Britain, U.S. polls showed that President Bush had the support of a clear majority of voters.

Americans might not have cleaved to the higher purpose of Bush's Operation Iraqi Freedom — to install democracy and unseat Saddam — if the president had not also pledged to do what years of United Nations weapons inspections had failed to do.

American troops would locate and destroy the chemical and biological weapons that the Bush administration claimed Saddam's henchmen had concealed. Behind every drumbeat of war was the implication that the poison — which Saddam had used to quell the Kurdish uprising in his own country — could be pointed at the United States.

With color-coded terrorist alerts in place

at home, Osama bin Laden on the loose and the other masterminds of the September 11 terrorist attacks on the United States still sending out "Death to America" videos to Al-Jazeera, most Americans bought the idea of preemptive war against a known enemy.

But almost two weeks into it, television images of Saddam — whether it really was Saddam or one of his doubles filled untold hours of debate — still stared belligerently back at the Americans from an undisclosed location. Even as some cable television experts started wondering if he might be dead, his loyalists fought on in a messy war. Chemical weapons were not being found.

Then, from the heartbreaking mess of the convoy ambush, gold was spun — first from an event that looked more dangerous on television than it perhaps had truly been, and next from a story of heroics in the fight at Nasiriyah that a Hollywood scriptwriter would have been hard put to invent.

"It had to happen," said Greg Jr. "I mean, look at that face. Who isn't going to fall in love with that face?"

After the rescue, U.S. officials released the eerie, dramatic, green-tinged night-vision video of the assault on Saddam General, which showed men at war bravely entering what seemed to be a hostile environment to bring out a wounded and help-less young soldier — a female soldier. United States soldiers had not rescued one of their own since World War II.

It would be a while before the whole story, a much better one, actually, would be told, of the doctors who treated her, of Jessi's fears and panic and a slow realization that the doctors and nurses were doing their best to help keep her alive.

It would be a while before the doctors and nurses in the hospital would say that there was no need for such force, that no one resisted, that the Fedayeen had left.

They were at war, U.S. officials pointed out. The halls had crawled with Fedayeen just hours before. Even as the commandos moved through Saddam General, American soldiers took fire just outside the hospital.

Uniforms meant nothing in this war. Most of the Americans who were killed in action died from bullets shot at them and grenades thrown at them by people in street clothes.

"Those guys *were* heroes," said Greg Lynch.

Everything he heard from Jessi's American doctors convinced him that, while she had been saved by the Iraqi doctors, she was failing and would have died if she had been left there, even if just a few days longer, in that wartime hospital.

She almost lost her leg once, he said. What would have happened to her if she had stayed a day or two more? Plus, there had always been the chance Jessica might be taken off to Baghdad, like other prisoners, so that she could be used by Saddam either as a trophy to rally his own support or as a way to weaken American support for the war. There was just too much uncertainty in both his daughter's condition and in the war that surrounded her even to suggest that what happened in the Iraqi hospital was not a rescue. He is grateful that the Iraqi doctors tried to save his daughter and that they tried to give her back, and he and Dee are sorry that the medical personnel were frightened by the commandos during the rescue.

"But she's my little girl," he said.

It is all the explaining he is willing to do.

But the mission's planners — and the Bush administration — would be castigated by critics of the war for what they considered a rank exploitation of the rescue.

"The rescue of Private Jessica Lynch, which inspired America during one of the most difficult periods of the war, was not the heroic Hollywood story told by the U.S. military," wrote *The Times* of London, "but a staged operation that terrified patients and victimized the doctors who had struggled to save her life, according to Iraqi witnesses."

The Times wrote that "four doctors and two patients, one of whom was paralyzed and on an intravenous drip, were bound and handcuffed as American soldiers rampaged through the wards, searching for departed members of the Saddam regime."

But American military officials, who made no apologies for sending in what they called "the door-kickers," said they never claimed that American soldiers took fire in the hospital.

Still, the perception, most of it created by the tape, was that Americans had fought their way in, and critics of the war would say that U.S. officials did not try hard enough to dispel that perception.

To assume that the commandos would have knocked politely at the hospital door is unrealistic, say the Lynches.

They barely care about the controversy, except in how it colors the legacies of the men who carried their daughter out of the hospital, and out of Iraq. They will always be grateful for that.

But the difference between perception and reality in what happened in the hospital with her rescuers was a sliver compared to the actions that would be attributed to Jessi in the battle itself. Less than one news cycle later, Jessi, damsel in distress, would be transformed into a kind of invincible action figure who absorbed bullets and just kept on fighting as the enemy closed in.

Newspapers all over the world ran this story from the Thursday, April 3, edition of *The Washington Post*:

Pfc. Jessica Lynch, rescued Tuesday from an Iraqi hospital, fought fiercely and shot several enemy soldiers after Iraqi forces ambushed the Army's 507th Ordnance Maintenance Company, firing her weapon until she ran out of ammunition, U.S. officials said.

Lynch, a 19-year-old supply clerk, continued firing at the Iraqis even after she sustained multiple gunshot wounds and watched several other soldiers in her unit die around her in fighting March 23, one official said . . . .

"She was fighting to the death," the official said. "She did not want to be taken alive."

Lynch was also stabbed when Iraqi forces closed in on her position, the official said, noting that initial intelligence reports indicated that she had been stabbed to death. No official gave any indication yesterday, however, that Lynch's wounds had been life threatening.

Several officials cautioned that the precise sequence of events is still being determined, and that further information will emerge as Lynch is debriefed. Reports thus far are based on battlefield intelligence, they said, which comes from monitored communications and from Iraqi sources in Nasiriyah whose reliability has yet to be assessed. Pentagon officials said they had heard "rumors" of Lynch's heroics but had no confirmation.

When Greg and Dee Lynch heard, they believed.

They knew their daughter was only about one hundred pounds, and they had to wonder how many bullets she could have possibly absorbed before falling, but they heard from Jessi's doctors in Germany that she had been shot more than once.

"I thought it could be true," Dee said. She believes that Jessi would have fought back and that she was terrified of being taken alive — that might have fueled the seemingly superhuman feats attributed to her.

They also believed because they are patriotic people from a patriotic place, and because they flew flags from the porch before Jessi was missing and because, after all they had been through, almost anything seemed possible.

And because they wanted to believe their daughter had hurt the enemy before they hurt her. And there was satisfaction in that, a kind of Old Testament justice in reverse.

They did not ask Jessi about it right away because they figured it might upset her, and because all they wanted in the world was for her to rest and heal and come home just as fast as possible. When reporters asked them about it, they usually said something trite: "Sounds like Jessi," as Dee said.

The myth lingered for days, transforming Jessi from the tragic wounded soldier to a warrior, a shining example of courage under fire. The military did not officially endorse it, but U.S. officials did not rapidly refute it, either, even after doctors reported that Jessi had not been shot, that the wounds they thought were bullet wounds were not.

Her Iraqi doctors said that she had not been shot, and in interviews with Western journalists, they scoffed at it as more fantasy and said her injuries were from a traffic accident.

It seemed that the story could not be anything except an extreme, that Jessi herself had to be either a hero or an utter fraud, even though she had never claimed to be a hero — had never claimed that she even pointed her rifle at anyone.

She cannot remember exactly when she heard about the stories being told about her, but she believes it was after leaving Landstuhl. Jessica told her mother and father then that her gun had jammed and that she had not shot anyone. She told her parents that the last thing she remembered was being in the Humvee with Lori, and bowing her head, and praying.

The headlines said SHE WAS FIGHTING TO THE DEATH.

"I didn't do that," she said.

"We didn't care," Dee said. "Not at all. All we cared about was getting her back."

Greg won't even consider the question, it's so irrelevant. The story of her made-for-television heroics, which began to evaporate almost as soon as he had heard it, gave grim satisfaction while it lasted. "I knew she was tougher than she looked," he said, and all the times he had said she was strong, that she was a survivor in all those front-porch interviews, was borne out.

He accepted the slaps on the back and the attaboys from his friends and relatives, but he said he was not disappointed in her when he found out it never happened. To Greg, Jessi showed more guts as she lay in that hospital bed, as she fought to save her leg from being cut off, than it would have taken to kill the men who were coming after her in the street.

"I'm proud of her," he said. "I was proud of her before I knew any of that stuff. She did something hard."

Jessi was not an action figure, but her life had been in genuine peril in that hospital, and her rescue, while not as dramatic as it had seemed, still came in the middle of a war and in a city where people were being routinely killed.

But some people believed Jessi, flat on her back in the hospital with catastrophic injuries, created her own myth, that she had tried to deceive others.

Her mother and father get angry over that, but Jessi just closes her eyes and shakes her head. "Don't they know I'd give anything in this world if it never happened at all?" she said.

She has more to say about it, but it makes her cry.

Helen Burns, like a lot of people in Wirt County, will not entertain for long the notion that Jessi was somehow responsible for the myths that swirled around her, and Helen almost had to run a man off for saying it.

"I had one guy come in after it was all over and he said it didn't really happen like they said it did, and that she wasn't shooting her way out at all, and he said the story's out now and now we'll finally know the truth," said Helen. "He said he didn't know why Jessi didn't tell the truth. And I told him Jessi didn't talk. Everyone else talked." Helen believes what a lot of people in Wirt County, and around the country, believe. She believes it is just foolish to blame Jessi for not being the kind of hero that the world believed she was, if even for just a few days.

If every hero were held to that standard, to that myth, say the people here, there wouldn't be any heroes. There would be only the Sergeant Yorks who shot down Germans like wild turkeys, and the young men who flung themselves on grenades.

"She was courageous to do what she done in the first place," said Helen. "I couldn't have done it. Everybody else was putting words in her mouth, but she never said nothing, and I don't hold that against her." How was she going to set the record straight from days of surgery and fleeting consciousness? "I'm proud of her. I think she did a good job anyway, going over there."

As Jessi lay in her hospital bed, she did not wonder about whether she was the kind of hero who deserved to be on the cover of *People* magazine, or whether there was a body count attached to the myth of her heroics in the ambush at Nasiriyah. She wondered why she could not feel anything below her waist. She wondered what had happened to the soldiers she saw slumped in the cabs of the crippled trucks. And she wondered about Lori. "Lori helped me get through the hospital in Nasiriyah," Jessi said. She knew Lori wasn't there, not really, but it was the idea of her, and Ruben and her family, who kept her hoping. Some days, she said, it had really seemed like Lori was sitting on the edge of the bed.

On the long flight over to Germany, Jessi had asked people on the plane about Lori, if they knew where she was, if she could talk to her. But no one would tell her anything — and she knew then that Lori was probably dead. She did not tell her mother and father on the phone that she knew, and they were afraid to mention Lori until they had to. So Jessi drifted in and out of her IV slumber with the increasing sense it was true, that Lori was really gone, because no one would even say her name.

Twenty-four

Not Knowing Who to Hate

The offering floated on the wind in Tuba
City. Percy Piestewa sprinkled a trail of corn-
meal on the air as she prayed, not for one
daughter, but two. "At six p.m., every day,"
Percy said. "It would have been daybreak in
Iraq."

For days she had prayed that the two
best friends would find nourishment in
that offering — and the strength to survive. It divined nothing. It was not a card
trick or crystal ball, just a prayer, older
than the country her daughter had gone
off to serve.

When Jessi was found, Percy rejoiced with
Dee. "She was so happy for us," Dee said.

Just a few days later, she got the news about Lori.

Even after Lori's death, she still prayed for Jessi. Her own daughter was gone, "and that was hard, so hard," Percy said. Morning by morning, she woke up to the realization that her daughter was dead, and every morning it was a surprise. "It always seemed like it had happened just the night before," she said.

When she prayed now, she still prayed for Lori, for her spirit, and for Jessi, because even though Jessi survived, she had been lost inside a dark cruelty. "I was sure it would take her a while to get back," she said.

Every day Greg and Dee Lynch spoke long-distance with Jessica and her doctors, and their peace of mind fluctuated as Jessi's fever rose and fell. Doctors at the Landstuhl hospital on the sprawling Ramstein Air Base worked to repair the injuries the Iraqi doctors had been unable even to address because of conditions and chaos at the wartime hospital, and at redoing some of the orthopedic reconstruction the surgeons had done.

Landstuhl surgeons realigned disks in her back and used metal plates to repair the fractures and relieve the pressure on nerves in her spine. Doctors told Dee and Greg that their work should return feeling to Jessica's lower legs. They reset the fractures in her legs and foot to give her a better chance at a more complete recovery.

"They put her back together with rods and plates and screws and pins," said Dee. "But they told me she would walk." It was just a matter of when, and how well. "The doctors couldn't give us a time span, but said it would only be a matter of time — it could be six months, or two years, or more."

But the nerve damage that had robbed Jessi of the control over her kidneys and bowels could not be so easily repaired, and Dee and Greg do not know if it ever can be.

Doctors also said, at the time, that Jessi bore two gunshot wounds — one to her arm, one to her leg — from what appeared to be small-caliber bullets, perhaps from a pistol. That diagnosis would change. The American doctors would later say Jessica was not wounded by gunfire, that the earlier assertions had been a mistake.

The wounds to her limbs, with splintered and protruding bone, had been a mess, but Dee and Greg still wonder why doctors said bluntly early in her treatment that Jessi had been shot, and then changed their minds.

Later, doctors would say that all her

broken bones probably came in the wreck of the Humvee, but that puzzles Dee and Greg, too. Some Iraqi doctors had said that Jessica seemed to have injuries consistent with having been stomped and beaten with rifle butts, and Dee and Greg wondered how she could be so badly broken in a crash the army estimated at about forty-five miles per hour on impact, when she had been in the rear compartment, wedged between the bodies of two soldiers and surrounded by duffel bags of equipment. "It just doesn't make sense," Greg said. How did the impact break bones on both sides of her body; how did that happen? Pictures of the Humvee had circulated in West Virginia newspapers — it had not looked badly damaged.

But it was better to believe it was just a wartime traffic accident, better to believe she was never subjected to the horrors that they heard about day after day of how Iraqi soldiers treated their captives.

At the time, Greg and Dee had only those fears — they did not know anything, had not seen any of her medical records, did not know what had happened in those three hours lost in Jessi's memory.

At the time, "we just wanted to go to her, to see her and be with her," Dee said. But they had to wait until the army's debriefing process was over, until Jessi had met with psychologists, until the army felt she was ready to be reunited with her family.

The celebration at home had faded into an infectious sense of well-being. The courthouse now wore a banner that read: JESSI IS FOUND. PRAISE THE LORD. REMEMBER OUR REMAINING TROOPS.

The post office was inundated, still. There were a hundred stuffed animals, a dozen crocheted flags, countless quilts and comforters, untold fuzzy blankets, battle uniforms from wars past, fruit baskets, candy and more cards and notes than the family, a houseful of cousins and volunteers from the sheriff's department could even try to open.

But all anyone talked about was the reunion with Jessi in Germany and when Jessi could come home.

Neither Greg nor Dee had worked since Jessi went missing. More than once, even with Jessi's fate still uncertain, he had thought about crawling into his truck and going out on the highway, because that was how he made a living. But he knew that, alone on the road with his thoughts and an eighteen-wheeler, he would drift across a yellow line or forget to go slow around a dead man's curve, killing himself and probably others. "There is no way I could have taken that truck out on those long runs with her on my mind. You forget for a minute in those things and you can hurt a whole lot of people." But mostly, he was just afraid of all that empty time, of being alone with his thoughts, of running through the possibilities of what had happened to her. "I knew I couldn't stand that," he said.

Donations had streamed in, in small checks from people all over America, giving them the means to make the trip. So Greg and Dee tried to figure out who could go, and when, and for how long.

Then, in a manifestation of goodwill that still leaves the Lynch family puzzled but grateful, a wealthy businessman just lent them a jet plane. Bill Johnson, chairman, president and CEO of H. J. Heinz, offered them a corporate jet so that the whole family could go to be with Jessi.

Once again, the gulf between their old life and this new celebrity found them a little unprepared. None of the Lynches had passports. They did not take European vacations. With the help of a senator, Democrat Jay Rockefeller of West Virginia, and Secretary of Defense Donald Rumsfeld, their passport applications were hurried through. On April 5, Greg, Dee, Greg Jr., Brandi and cousin Dan Little drove to Yeager Airport in the capital city of Charleston.

At the airport, Greg and Dee stepped up to a microphone for one last press conference.

"I can't wait to see her," Dee said.

"I feel real good," Greg said.

During the question-and-answer, a reporter asked if Greg knew that bodies found in Iraq had been identified as the other missing soldiers from the 507th convoy.

All week, the family had avoided the news. They had focused all their attentions on Jessi. Greg was an old hand by now at press conferences — he had done so many he knew what to say and how to say it. With practice, people get good at their grief.

He sounded like a diplomat at first.

"I wasn't aware of this," he said. "Our hearts are really saddened for her other troop members and the other families."

But Greg could not stomach it anymore. The truck driver from Palestine thought about dead soldiers, about polite men in uniform walking up driveways to tell parents that their sons and daughters would not be coming home again, and about how, for them, there would be no miracle. And he realized there was no right thing to say, and he began to cry.

"I can't do this no more," he said to a young man named Randy Coleman, a state public relations director who had been handling the press conference.

"I can't," Greg said.

He boarded the plane, the big, fancy jet that he was so happy to have, and flew away with his family to visit a daughter who should have been dead but was not.

Nine hours later, their jet touched down at Ramstein Air Base. They were taken to the hospital, and they walked down a hallway where heroes lay inside every half-open doorway.

The Lynches stopped just outside Jessi's room, a tiny, intensive care room that, from the outside, seemed to be mostly machines, with one small, bandaged bit of flesh and blood in the middle.

"I brought a camcorder, to record it so that one day Jessi could show it to her kids," said Dan Little, a first sergeant in the West Virginia National Guard. "I couldn't do it.

"All my life, I've heard about the two-hundred-yard stare, and I saw it for the first time in the eyes of a nineteen-year-old girl," he said. "I expected the worst, but the look in her eyes haunted me. I couldn't look at it, even through that lens."

He turned the camcorder off.

And Little thought, "What we had feared, the most we had feared, was not enough."

There was silence in the room for a few seconds. Jessi was much thinner than they remembered, and her head had been shaved so doctors could better treat her head wound. Dee stood transfixed by the sight of so many machines, so many tubes and wires, by the bag of blood that hung near her daughter's bed. She knew that what she was seeing in the bed was no worse than what any mother saw after a child's catastrophic accident — in fact, all through this ordeal Dee had told herself that she was not special, that the pain, fear and worry were spread out over the American landscape, coming home to people who lived with as much or worse, much worse. As she looked at her daughter she was determined not to cry, but she could not speak, either.

"Oh my God," she said, inside her head.

Greg could not talk, either, nor did Brandi.

Jessi looked at them and smiled.

Greg Jr. took a step into the room.

"Poomba," she said.

The family moved carefully around the bed.

"We just wanted to touch her," Dee said.

She looked right into her daughter's face and lied. "You look good," she said.

Dee asked her to open her mouth.

"I just wanted to make sure she still had all her teeth," Dee said. "They were fine."

Greg Jr. smiled at her and joked, but all he could think about was somehow, anyhow, striking back at the people who had done this to her. As he hugged her, he thought about choking them, and the hate rose up in him like bile.

"And I couldn't do nothin'," he said.

So he smiled, just smiled.

"I was as sad as when I heard that she was missing," he said, because, in a way, she still was. "It broke my heart. She was broken, helpless."

He thought about the times they had played army, about the day they had enlisted — he always thought, despite all that pap about seeing the world, she did it just because she still wanted to compete with him, the same reason she'd entered that damn steer in the county fair when everyone knew Jessi didn't know a steer from a sensible shoe.

"It should have been me lying there," he said.

Brandi looked at the figure on the bed and wondered where her sister was.

"She wasn't Jessi," Brandi said.

"Her voice was so whiny, so soft, like she was a baby again," Brandi said. "She tried to joke, but . . ."

Dan Little stood back a little, the switched-off camera in his hands.

He has a daughter, too. He looked at Greg, who stood laughing and joking beside his daughter and never let on for one second the shock and dismay that had gripped him as he walked in and looked down at her. Little marveled at it, how he did it.

They talked, gently, about what had happened to her.

Dee said Jessi talked about the battle at Nasiriyah and about the civilian hospital, but did not talk to her at all about Lori or about what had happened between the ambush and her awakening three hours later in the military hospital.

The only injuries they knew about were the ones they could see covered in bandages or held together with sutures.

A few days after the family arrived in Germany, Jessi's psychologist, Lieutenant Colonel Sally Harvey, met with Greg and Dee in Jessi's room to tell them what she could about what had happened in those lost hours.

"She wanted us to be there when she told Jessi," Dee said.

Dee stood beside Jessi's bed and held her good hand, and Greg stood on the other side of the bed, his hand resting on her. Col. Harvey told them that Jessi had been assaulted, and of the injuries resulting from that savagery.

Jessi's face did not change.

"She just lay there, and her face was blank," said Dee.

She thought Jessi might at least grip her hand harder, something, but her hand was limp.

"She was numb. She was on a lot of medication. Maybe that was it," Dee said.

Jessi acted as if it were something that had happened to someone else, someone she didn't know.

"I don't remember," she said, turning her face up to look at her mother. "I don't know."

Dee kept waiting for her to just break down.

She is still waiting.

"She didn't cry," Dee said. "They couldn't get her to cry."

Dee leaned over her daughter's face.

"It's okay," she said. "You don't think about it. You don't have to think about it."

Later, doctors would say it would be better for Jessi if she could cry about it, if she could face it, but Dee is not sure about that. If Jessi wants to keep those hours in a dark place, a place darker than the deepest mine, then her mother will stand guard at the entrance to that place, all her life if need be, waiting. She does not know what she will do if it ever comes out.

Maybe it never will.

"And I will thank God for that," she said.

Greg stood and listened to the lieutenant colonel and watched his daughter's face.

Nothing.

Just the green eyes, blank and staring.

Later, he walked out in the hall.

"Who do I hate?" he said. "If I could have got my hands on them, if I could have got at 'em, but I couldn't. I would never get to do that. And you can't hate a whole country.

"Some of 'em was good to Jessi. You can't hate a whole people."

It is odd, the way the Lynches approached their daughter's recovery then, and now. At the time, all they sent home to West Virginia and the United States was good and hopeful news.

It was almost like their patriotism prevented them from sending home any bad news. But Dee was still afraid. "Jessi's main nutrition was a few sips of Ensure, a nutritional drink. But no, she never ate much. When she tried to eat, she got sick."

It was reported that she had moved from her bed to a chair and was sitting up, laughing with family and doctors, playing on the computer.

"It took five people to move me from my bed," Jessi said.

For Dee, it was perhaps the most conflicting time in her life. "I was scared but so happy," she said. "Mostly, I just wanted to go home, to take Jessi and go home."

Jessi was in the hospital almost two weeks before doctors decided she was strong enough to be transferred to Walter Reed Army Medical Center in Washington, D.C.

On April 12, Jessi was one of fifty wounded soldiers who were carried or helped aboard a massive C-17 Globemaster cargo plane. Thick blankets hid their wounds, so it was hard to tell who had suffered what. "Just all these broken boys," Dan Little said.

"You could hear this groaning, and you knew they were in so much pain," Dee said. The Lynches and family members of the other soldiers took seats closer to the front of the plane for the nine-hour flight. From time to time, one of the soldiers who could walk would come by and ask the family about Jessica, and some walked over to Jessi to say hello.

But she was asleep, almost always asleep, she said.

She never could stay awake on a long trip. On the flight to Kuwait, she and Lori had buckled in and started to talk, waiting for the free food to arrive. The great thing about a long flight, they had heard, was that the army bombarded the soldiers with snacks, as if in some kind of compensation for all the stale and dusty Meals Ready to Eat they would have to squeeze and pour from plastic pouches. But before the first snack was tossed their way both of them had drifted off, leaning on each other, and they had awakened hours later, the flight almost over, a pile of sandwiches in their laps.

Twenty-five

Changes

Jessi had not looked in the mirror since she had glanced in the side mirror of her truck in the Iraqi desert. She refused to look in the mirror at Landstuhl and, at first, at Walter Reed, Dee said. "When she was a little girl, everything had to be so perfect, had to be precise," Dee said. "And here she is just trying to get a spoon to her mouth, and her hand is shaking, getting it all over herself. We'd feed her. No, she never looked in the mirror."

The nerve damage in her arm had improved at Landstuhl, but she still could not do simple things, like hold a spoon or turn loose of it when she was done eating, and she would stare, wondering, at the things that just stuck like flypaper to her hand.

"She couldn't wring out a washrag and hold it to her face," Dee said. "I washed her face, like when she was little."

Jessi did not cry then, either, or throw a tantrum, her mother said. She just kept trying. They kept wondering when she would cry, hoping for it, believing that when it came, it would be some kind of release. At least, that is the way it is in the movies.

But when Jessi did finally cry, it was only because she found a new depth to her despair. Doctors had hoped that a device similar to a heart pacemaker could be used to stimulate her kidneys, giving her some control over her bladder.

"They told her she had a seventy percent chance," Dee said.

The procedure failed.

"She cried then," Dee said.

But slowly, her mom said, Jessi began to get better in other ways. Her legs began to regain some feeling, and her hand got stronger. Soon after coming to Walter Reed, Jessi was fighting to get back what she had lost.

From time to time, she even laughed. She would feel her head, feel the short hair that sprouted there and the bald patch around her head wound.

The doctors had not cut the back of her hair, so she had, by July, what seemed to be a 1970s punk-rock haircut. "I had a mullet," she said. "I was Joe Dirt."

There was no rigorous physical therapy, not yet. She just sat in a chair, after being helped into it, and worked to regain the use of her hand. As the wounds healed, therapists worked her legs for her, and later she began to take steps on her walker and crutches.

Dee would stand off to one side and watch her daughter struggle. Later, Ruben got leave and came to visit, and he became her cheerleader. They had finally gotten to see each other in the hospital. Callers had to know a patient code to get through Jessi's security. Theirs was "Taco Bell Number 4" — after what they had ordered at the drive-through when they were first dating. When she wanted to give up, he chided her. Her family was so gentle, so worried, she needed someone like Ruben, she said, to keep her working through the pain.

For Jessi, it was simple. She wanted back what she had before. She did not want to dance ballet or play concert piano. She wanted to walk to the movies through a mall, wanted to press a gas pedal and steer herself to the Taco Bell drive-through.

She wanted to go to college and be a kindergarten teacher and hold babies. She also had another picture in her mind. She would walk down an aisle and get married, though Ruben had not worked up the nerve to tell her father they had talked about marriage and that he had given Jessi a promise ring. Greg had shot at three men in West Virginia over a can of gas and fully intended to shoot one more, someday, over his wounded dog. What would he do if he thought he was going to lose his daughter? But in Jessi's mind she could see the wedding. "I really wanted to be able to walk at that," Jessi said.

At Walter Reed, as at Landstuhl, Jessi's family stayed in apartments at the Fisher House, which provided the families of some soldiers a place to stay just steps from the army hospital. They were at her bedside every minute they were allowed between surgeries and rehab, although the likelihood that Jessi would die from her wounds had faded.

All she talked about now was going home.

Jessi's return to the United States had only whipped up interest in her story, both from the people who had fallen in love with her and the people who saw her as a pawn in a presidential administration's plan to sell the war to the American people.

When she arrived at Walter Reed in mid-April, U.S. officials still held that the use of the video of her rescue was appropriate — and maintained that the Special Forces commandos who rescued her acted bravely and correctly in the middle of a war zone by going full-tilt into the hospital. In fact, they never would accept a BBC report's conclusion that the Americans fabricated their own *Black Hawk Down* drama in order to sell the war, an opinion others, in the media and the public, would adopt.

Jessi is glad that the army never backed away from its portrayal of the commandos as anything less than heroes. It makes her angry that people, safe in their living rooms, who never had to be frightened by the sound of gunfire as they watched the war unfold on TV, would question the bravery it took to go into a building that was a known headquarters of the Fedayeen. "They saved me. They did. They're the heroes." She points out that one out of every three members of the 507th convoy is now dead, soldiers who never expected to be in combat.

She knows she is no expert on wars. But she knows that there was no real safe place in Nasiriyah. As for the hospital, every door could have held a Fedayeen with an AK-47. Who would knock on that door?

One man with an automatic weapon could have killed the whole rescue team as they carried Jessi through the hallway and down the stairwell. "They could have shot us all in the back," she said.

She knows that the Iraqi doctors and nurses tried to give her back. But that failed. "If I had stayed I would have died," she said. "I wasn't eating or going to the bathroom." And although the nurses and doctors were kind to her and did their best to keep her alive, Jessi felt that they had done all they could. She still wonders if she would have a leg to rehabilitate if she had been left in that overtaxed Iraqi hospital, despite the devoted doctors — or if she would even be alive.

She understands the controversy, but dismisses it. She does not expect everyone to see the urgency in her situation. It was not their life, and not their leg.

But the army had not rushed to officially challenge that original, faulty, off-the-record image of Jessi as a death-dealing warrior. Jessi, flat on her back, in surgery or in recovery every day, could not do it for them. "Jessica didn't even know what was being said," Dee said, anger rising in her voice at the notion that Jessica should have spoken out from her tangle of blood bags and IV drips.

The Lynches — with two children in uniform, one of them being operated on by surgeons in a military hospital after being rescued by elite military commandos — did not speak out against the military even after Jessi said, in a voice still weak from her wounds, that she never fired her gun. It was not their place. They waited for the army's official report on the ambush, due out in July 2003, and for Jessi herself to feel well enough to tell them what had really happened.

The report spelled out the less sensational — but no less terrifying — version of her role in the ambush. But it left many family members of the killed soldiers unsatisfied. The report told of Captain King's missed and wrong turns, but some family members felt the army had held no one accountable.

"Soldiers fight as they are trained to fight," the army investigators wrote in an executive summary of the report. "Once engaged in battle, the Soldiers of the 507th Maintenance Company fought hard. They fought the best they could until there was no longer a means to resist. They defeated ambushes, overcame hastily prepared enemy obstacles, defended one another, provided life-saving aid and inflicted casualties on the enemy. The Soldiers of the 507th upheld the Code of Conduct and followed the Law of War."

Over the days ahead, Jessi's condition slowly improved. She was able to stand and finally able to take a step, but only if most of her weight was being supported by someone else or by a walker.

The day before she left for home, a small group of family, friends, doctors, nurses and a few patients gathered in an auditorium inside the hospital. Her family helped her into her dress uniform and wheeled her in.

With help, she stood.

Lieutenant General James B. Peake, the army surgeon general, pinned three medals on her uniform.

A Purple Heart, for her wounds.

A Prisoner of War medal, for her ordeal.

And a Bronze Star, for meritorious service in combat.

Her mother and father were proud.

Then, with help, she sank back down in her wheelchair.

"They can have it all back," Dee said. "They can have the medals, all that publicity, everything, if I can have her back the way she was."

That night, Jessi sat in a chair. She brushed her hair. The brush stayed in her hand. When she tried to put it down, her hand worked, it did what her mind told it to.

For the thousandth time, Dee looked at her and thought how lucky she was.

"The Iraqi forces in Nasiriyah conducted fierce attacks against the convoy," the investigators of the ambush wrote. "Of the 33 U.S. Soldiers in the convoy, 11 were killed in combat or died as a result of injuries, 7 were captured by Iraqi forces, and the remaining 16 Soldiers were able to rejoin friendly forces. Of the 22 U.S. Soldiers who survived, 9 were wounded in action. Although all details of the battle could not be determined with certainty, it is clear that every U.S. Soldier did their duty."

That day, with her medals on her dress uniform, Jessi looked in the mirror, then at her mother.

"I want to go home," she said.

Twenty-six

Barn Raising

Almost from the day that people in Wirt County heard about the extent of Jessi's wounds, the sound of hammers began to bang through the hollow on Mayberry Run Road. Friends, family and neighbors worked their regular shifts and then drove to the Lynches' home to work another eight hours, and more. People used vacation time, called in sick or took the loss on their paychecks and came to work on the old house anyway, because this was not some helpless vigil where they were at the mercy of events on the other side of the globe. This was something they could affect, something they could measure, cut to fit and nail down.

Junior Collins, Greg's truck driver buddy, is not much of a talker anyway. He had been helpless to do anything when Jessi was a captive, and he never knew what to say. Now the scream of a Skil saw said all that needed to be said.

It was a barn raising, really. Men came walking into the yard with tool belts around their waists, or drove up with donated lumber, nails and cement blocks.

Jessi's life had changed, and they had to change the house to fit her, to make the rooms easier for a person in a wheelchair, with a walker or on crutches to steer through.

It started with a few friends sitting around, just thinking. The little house had been built to fit the rough land, full of steps and split-levels. They thought, "You know, Jessi's gonna have a hard time gettin' up them steps." It ended with cement trucks backing down the driveway, men crawling over the outer walls like worker ants, and a house that would nearly double in size.

Donations — of money, materials, appliances and man hours — poured in, at first just to provide wheelchair access to the house for Jessi and provide her with a bedroom and bathroom that were handicap-accessible. The work was donated by the people here, but the money was donated from folks around the country, more than fifty thousand dollars by the time Jessi returned from Germany.

In just a few days, the good intentions of a few close friends had ballooned into "Jessi's Home Project" — with a sign and everything. Lew Peck and Duane Edwards, a couple of friends who just wanted to do something nice for the family while they were at Landstuhl with Jessi, led as many as fifteen volunteers a day at the house.

Greg had known that friends might lend a hand or a favor to make things better for Jessi when she came home, but when he and Dee came back from Walter Reed for Brandi's high school graduation, they found a half-built expansion that transformed their little home into Dee's dream house.

"It's the house I always wanted," Dee said. "It's the kitchen I always wanted. I had closets. I loved it, every bit of it. And then I felt bad, because of the reason I had it."

They even had to hold another press conference.

Greg had been assuming the spokesperson role most of the time, especially since Greg Jr. had returned to duty. This time it was Brandi who faced the press.

"While our family has been with Jessi in Germany and in Washington, friends at home have invested their time, their money and their hearts," said Brandi, as the cameras rolled.

If the Lynches went to get a quart of milk, the cameras rolled.

"Our family is blessed to have been born in Wirt County, West Virginia," Brandi said, with eight microphones in front of her face.

The words were written on notepaper. The Lynches were all good, by now, at talking to the press, at saying the right thing. But Greg said his family could not have meant those words any more if they had burned them into the wood of the new walls or written them in wet concrete.

He was grateful but not surprised. Wirt County had always been the kind of place where, when a person asked if there was anything he could do to help, that question was a lot more than rhetorical.

"People gave up their own jobs," Greg said, "to come and do this for her. They gave up their own families to do this."

They had gotten bored with standing around, looking glum and drinking up all the Lynches' coffee, anyway. Benny Smith, who is married to Janice, the relative who wanted to drown Greg Jr. as a child, turned screws on a new set of porch lights.

"Is it straight?" he said.

"Let me look," Greg said.

He walked off a few feet and cocked his head a little, to compensate.

"Yep," he said.

Benny smiled.

"But it ain't high enough," Greg said.

Benny redid it.

It was high enough then.

But it wasn't straight.

"Shit," Benny said.

Greg turned his back and smiled. Even though their kindness made him proud of the place he was from and the people he had grown up with, it was a little sad to see the transformation take place. Every time he returned from Jessi's side, first from Landstuhl, then from Walter Reed, the house looked less and less like the home he had left.

Greg Lynch had loved the little A-frame house the first time he saw it, when he was still a boy. It fit the hollow the way a star fits a Christmas tree, and he sweated over hammers and shovels and shifted a million gears to pay for it.

He planned to raise his family, grow old and die in it. It was more than good enough for him, it was just right. He took pictures of it, in case anything ever happened to it, a fire or a bad storm.

But instead, it was swallowed by goodwill.

It was as if, once people got started doing something that made them feel good, they couldn't stop — or they just didn't want to.

Jessi would be in a wheelchair for months at least, and unable to walk without her walker or crutches for more months, if not years — and even after she was walking, a fall could be catastrophic. So the carpenters — here, just about every man knows how to use a level and swing a hammer and owns his own power tools — set to work enlarging the first floor.

They built a spacious bedroom on the ground floor with an adjoining bathroom — all of it handicap-accessible. They installed a special bathtub with handrails and a seat.

It could have ended there.

"People just kept helping," Greg Jr. said.

The one-story house became a two-story house, with a bedroom for Dee and Greg, a bedroom for Greg Jr., and a bedroom for Brandi, all on the second floor.

The stairway now climbs to an atrium and a computer room. Furniture just appeared, as if by magic. Jessi got a fancy adjustable bed, to help with her circulation. The house had never had central heat and air; workers installed it. And they added two bathrooms.

Outside, a gully in the front yard was filled in and the driveway enlarged so that any car ferrying Jessi could pull right up to the door. Masons laid a big, block retaining wall on the hill next to the house, to keep the mountain at bay.

And on the second floor, they built a wraparound balcony so that the family can sit and watch the evening. Friends and neighbors filled the refrigerators and pantries with food, and the drawers with candy.

It was not cheap work, not prefab anything. The honey-colored wood trim in the kitchen gleamed. Workers took the old microwave to the new media room — complete with a big television — and installed in the kitchen the big, fancy black one, which looks a little bit like it was taken from a starship, and is about that hard to operate.

Greg punched buttons on it once, one after another, like he expected it to play a tune. "If I need to heat something, I use the old one," he said.

One night, as the construction neared completion, Greg sat with Dee on the balcony — people here just call it a porch — and felt the breeze. The fireflies wobbled on the air, and the bugs of early summer had just started to flutter and hum.

"If it was Saturday night," Greg said, "we'd turn on the bug zapper, and watch it go to town."

Twenty-seven

Home

Arol C. Squires dusted off his uniform and got ready for the parade. He had served in Korea as a young man and, like others at the V.F.W., he was proud to be an honor guard one more time. "They live back in these hollers and they just want to get away," he said of the generations of young people who left here for the army, navy and marines. Over his lifetime, he has seen them come home on crutches, in wheelchairs and in zipped-up plastic bags, but he has never seen one of them come home in such a way as this.

"I'd like to see them all come back like this," he said.

His part of West Virginia had always been

kind to soldiers — it had been wrapped in yellow ribbon before. But this time, as Wirt County and beyond prepared for the homecoming of its most famous soldier, the place almost hummed with patriotism.

"A good day," he said.

It was never a place of pretensions. People here wore blue jeans to funerals — it was the showing up that mattered, not what kind of britches you had on as you walked past the casket. They are proud to be from Two Run, Round Bottom and Society Hill, and they eat white bread because it tastes better. But as the days to Jessica's homecoming dwindled, this place — cities, towns, hamlets and wide places in the road — reached deep into the closet and pulled out its church clothes.

This was no simple red carpet. It took highway equipment and work crews to get this corner of West Virginia ready, to its citizens' satisfaction, to welcome home a daughter who had been through hell on earth on the other side of the hollow. Her welcome home would be perfect.

A giant billboard went up in Parkersburg, devoted to her on the off chance that she might, as her helicopter swooped over, see it from the air.

But here in Wirt County, in particular,

the citizens readied for that arrival with an excitement and a pride that was unprecedented. "The biggest thing ever to happen to Wirt County," everyone said. A few crotchety skeptics spouted that Jessi really had not done a thing to deserve this hero's welcome, but the rest of the population just gave them a good, long, go-to-hell look and ignored them.

Workmen laid a brand-new coat of black, shiny sealant on the parking lot at Dick's Market in Elizabeth. After years of cussing and rattling over cracked asphalt, drivers found that Mayberry Run Road had a fresh new repaving. "They even tried to widen it a little bit," said Greg Lynch. "Did a pretty good job."

There was not a high weed or a candy wrapper to mar the roadsides in the town of Elizabeth, and at the baseball field where Jessi's helicopter was expected to land, the road was spread with fresh gravel.

On the courthouse lawn, inmates on a work detail from the regional jail cut the grass and prettied things up, and houses on roads into Elizabeth and Palestine carried homemade signs that promised her that her journey was over:

YOU'RE ALMOST HOME, JESSI

The fact she was flying in did not matter a bit.

On the eve of the homecoming, the bang of hammers and the whine of electric saws continued into the night as the volunteer carpenters raced the clock to finish work on the Lynch family's house.

In Elizabeth, high school students pasted bumper stickers on their cars that read JESSI IS A WIRT COUNTY TIGER. By the eve of the homecoming, some ten thousand T-shirts — WELCOME HOME, JESSI — had been sold from local stores.

At a lovely, tree-lined park on the Little Kanawha River, a media village, crowded with satellite trucks, had been set up. Nearby, a circus tent had been erected where Jessi would address the press and — through them — the country, and technicians had laid cables and strung phone lines. Reporters from around the world had called for credentials; more than 350 had entered the gate to the media area by the morning of her homecoming.

Joseph Carey, director of strategic communications for West Virginia Governor Bob Wise, had been an advance man for Bill Clinton, but he'd never seen anything like this. They came to hear a young woman sit and read a few minutes of rehearsed speech, and take no questions.

The last time something big was supposed to happen here, it never did. Because of that French and Indian War, Wirt County had not become a pushing-off place for the colonies' expansion west.

This time, they were taking no chances. State troopers and other law enforcement officers prowled the streets in patrol cars, cruised the river in patrol boats and roamed the hills and woods on four-wheelers.

By dawn of the homecoming, special antiterrorism soldiers were in place around the town of Elizabeth and even in the woods behind the Lynches' house.

"Anticipation in this just grew and grew, beyond belief," said Randy Coleman, the communications director for the West Virginia Department of Military Affairs and Public Safety, who had become a press spokesman for the family and helped write the speech Jessica would give. Coleman would become the family spokesman on many issues and would get to know the family as well as any nonrelative or old friend.

"I wonder if the kid herself could have even imagined how big this was," Coleman said.

By noon, people were already putting

lawn chairs out on the parade route, a mix of locals, almost-locals (from across the Ohio River) and folks who had driven for hours to be a part of history.

"Just to see her," said Harold Marshall, the retired windshield maker, who drove in from Vienna. "It could go on for years," he said of the war in Iraq. "But we got her back."

Brady and Jane Huffman drove over from Middleport, Ohio, for the same reason. "We just wanted to be here," said Brady, "to see with our own eyes that she got back."

"I wish they all had got back," Jane said.

The idea that some people would criticize this, see it as excess, offended them. "What she went through? I don't think she should have to do anything more for the rest of her life," Brady said.

At about 2 p.m., a Black Hawk helicopter curved in the sky overhead.

"Is that her?" people asked.

Schoolchildren unfurled a huge American flag — big as a coal truck — and flapped it up and down, hoping she would see.

The next day, in *The Herald-Dispatch* newspaper, they learned that she had. "If it wasn't for her ears, her smile would have cut her head in half," said Staff Sergeant Paula

Tucker, a flight medic who flew in with Jessi, in a front-page story in that newspaper.

The Black Hawk, carrying Jessi, her parents, her cousin Dan Little and Ruben from Washington, D.C., touched down at the baseball field at about 2 p.m. She was driven to a tent, where female relatives surrounded her, cooing and fussing, and went to work on her hair and makeup.

They dusted specks off her immaculate, dark green dress uniform, straightened her black beret.

Jessi, even when she smiled at relatives she had not seen for a year, still looked stricken. Her back throbbed, her legs — the parts of them that she could feel — ached. And her foot, the one held together with a metal screw, alternated between dead and tingly. Doctors had given her morphine to dull the pain of the trip, but she was mostly alert and by now anxious to face the public for the first time. But she had imagined a much smaller homecoming than this. "I never expected there to be so many people," she said. "I was terrified."

Her mother and father say a lot of people forget that Jessi left Palestine as a just-graduated high school senior who had never seen much of the world that you couldn't get to in a four-wheel-drive Toyota. She came home not just broken but famous, besieged by well-meaning people, by the press, and thrust into a spotlight — and into a political controversy — that almost anyone would have found overwhelming. "None of us had ever been through anything like this — and I don't know anybody who ever had," said Dee. Jessi had never made a speech outside English class. Now she was making one covered by Swedish television, British newspapers and NPR.

As Helen Burns had said, people had been talking for Jessi for months, and even though it was just a prepackaged statement, it still contained only the things that she wanted to say with her own voice. It was important to her to sound good and to look good. But as showtime crept closer she felt a little bit like her whole mind and body were held together by the brass buttons on her uniform — and she was so afraid she would stutter and stammer and sound like a doofus. She should have known by then, after untold letters, cards, presents and hand-me-down medals, that no one would have laughed at her or thought less of her if she had leaned toward the microphone and fallen face-first on the floor. But instead, what was going through Jessi's mind, on the eve of one of the most anticipated events since the war began, was, "Oh, crap. I'm a deer in the headlights."

Her father stood just outside the tent and stared at the people who lined both sides of Highway 14. "I didn't think this little town could hold so many people," he said. "It was just astonishing."

Her speech would be heard by the media, family and friends. Then she would ride through the town in an old-fashioned parade, through the tiny downtown and past stands selling homemade lemonade and one-dollar cheeseburgers.

The plan was for Jessi to memorize the brief statement, a speech she had worked on for hours with Randy Coleman.

"We worked so hard on it. I rehearsed it so much, so I would know it by heart," said Jessi.

"As soon as I walked in there, and saw all those cameras and all those lights and all those people, I just forgot everything," she said.

First, Governor Wise welcomed the media and the world to her homecoming. It was a moment of import, and even though Jessi's homecoming had to be — because of the sheer numbers of media and well-wishers — a staged, well-orchestrated media event, it required a speech not only of pomp but of poetry.

"We welcome back a young citizen and soldier, a symbol of the quiet courage and commitment of all our armed services," said Wise. "Our entire state has worn a yellow ribbon around its heart.

"We mourn and remember the loss of your comrades," he said.

"But God," he said, "is still in the business of miracles and one of his miracles has come home to the mountains."

Greg Jr., also in dress uniform, introduced his sister. He said he had believed that Jessi was supposed to look up to him, as her older brother, but now he looked up to her.

In a trailer, just before the speech, he had been less loving. "Shoot, man, she's got a Bronze Star," he said, and rolled his eyes.

Jessica sat in her wheelchair and, against the backdrop of another massive American flag, gazed out into the rows of poised pens, and was scared to death.

After everything she had been through, the idea of talking in front of so many people all but froze her mind. She had so wanted to just say her speech, to make it seem as she meant it, from her heart.

"I just had to read it," she said.

Even though she was trembling ever so

faintly in her chair, she was smiling and appeared calmer than she really was. The thing she hated most was that she could not stand. She had wanted to walk even a few steps to the lectern and show the people who cared about her around the country that she was getting better. But she could not.

"Hi. Thank you for being here. It's great to be home.

"I would like to say thank you to everyone who hoped and prayed for my safe return. For a long time I had no idea so many people knew I'd been missing. But I read thousands of letters, many of them from children, who offered messages of hope and faith. I would like to thank the people in this community, especially those who gave donations to the Lynch fund and who volunteered their time and skills to work on my family's house.

"Please allow me to thank the doctors, nurses and staff members of Walter Reed Army Medical Center for the excellent care they gave me. I would like to thank the staff of Landstuhl Medical Center in Germany for their care and support. I would like to thank the Fisher Foundation, Governor Bob Wise and United States Senator Jay Rockefeller for the roles they played in helping my family to be with me in Germany and Washington. I am also grateful to several Iraqi citizens who helped save my life while I was in their hospital — and a unit of our Special Forces who saved my life.

"I want to thank Sergeant Ruben Contreras," and with that Jessi looked up from the shaking sheaf of paper and looked at Ruben. "You never let me give up. When I wanted to quit P.T. [physical therapy], you kept me going. And you're my inspiration and I love you.

"I'm proud to be a soldier in the army. I'm proud to have served with the 507th. I'm happy that some of the soldiers I served with made it home alive, and it hurts that some of my company didn't. Most of all, I miss Lori Piestewa. She was my best friend. She fought beside me and it was an honor to have served with her. Lori will always remain in my heart.

"I read thousands of stories that said when I was rescued, I said, 'I'm an American soldier, too.' Those stories were right. Those were my words. I am an American soldier, too."

She thanked the people there, told them it was good to be home and was wheeled out, to applause. Even reporters clapped.

"Beautiful, baby," said Joe Carey, the veteran advance man who had put the show together. "Clinton? Yeltsin? This is the best dance I've ever done."

Jessi was lifted from her wheelchair and eased onto the back of a red Mustang convertible. The last time she had ridden in a parade she'd stood on her own two feet and waved to the people of her town, who had looked up and seen just a pretty face, just a girl who went to school with their girls. Now she was the hero, whatever that meant. She was the girl who had been beaten and brutalized and rescued in the middle of a war, who came home to magazine covers and morphine, to movie offers and physical therapy.

Greg Jr. sat beside her on the back of the Mustang. Jessi rested her bad arm on Ruben, who sat in the front seat, and waved to the crowd with her uninjured arm. People lined the road, cheering, throwing kisses, waving signs — STAMFORD, TEXAS, SAYS WELCOME HOME, JESSICA, and WE LOVE YOU.

"My foot hurt so bad, and my back, from sitting," she said. But she had been helpless for so long, she wanted to pretend for a little while — even if just for a car ride — that everything was going to be just fine, everything could be just like it had been.

So she just rode, and waved, and smiled.

Twenty-eight

Normal?

With every breeze, the house rippled in red, white and blue.

It was covered in flags. They snapped from a wraparound porch and an upstairs balcony, flew from the radio antennas of cars that crowded the driveway, rode on the T-shirts of men who hugged her when she was pushed into the renovated house.

It was a more quiet celebration, this July homecoming, than when she was first found. Then, it was enough to know she was alive. "We never stopped laughing," said her grandmother Wyonema.

Now the wheelchair rolled into the house and showed them the awful gray area between black and white, something that no amount of red, white and blue would cover over.

Jessi worked hard at her rehabilitation. Now she tried to walk without a walker, crutches or help. In a few weeks, she took a step and a half, and a few weeks later she took five steps. In late September she took thirty-eight steps.

It was not a Cinderella story.

But her mother, father, sister and brother tried to make it that way. If Jessi wanted spaghetti at midnight, they put on a pot of water. Like a little girl, home from the doctor's office after having her appendix out, she was surrounded by toys and candy. But she took morphine tablets with her M&Ms, and when she asked her mom to sleep with her, it was because her legs hurt so bad she could not stand to be alone.

Outside the house, people still rushed to do nice things. The state promised her full scholarships to any West Virginia school, for her and her two siblings. "Some people brought covered dishes," said Governor Wise. "This is what we did."

Presents continued to rain in, from boxes of blue jeans to promises of a new car. Long after the myth of her gunplay in the battle had evaporated, cards, letters and boxes flooded the post office. In time it became clear that most Americans did not care if Jessi had emptied her magazine in a battle with the enemy or not — it was what Jessica had lived through that was important, not how many lives she took or if she took life at all. It was not spin. Letters, by the thousands, said so, letters from people who supported the war and from people who did not.

She should have been a poster child for the war, but for Jessi the war was too personal for that.

"We went and we did our job, and that was to go to the war, but I wish I hadn't done it — I wish it had never happened," she said, as she sat in her wheelchair in her mom's kitchen — her pills, just six this time, lined up in front of her on the kitchen table. "I wish we hadn't been there, none of us. I wish . . . I dunno.

"I don't care about the political stuff. But if it had never happened, Lori would be alive and all the rest of the soldiers would be alive. And none of this," she said, meaning her wheelchair, her scars, "would have happened."

She does not read a lot of newspapers or magazines, but she knows that some people say she does not deserve the attention she got — and does not even deserve the kindnesses she has received. Some people will never forgive her for not being rescued in a hail of gunfire, for not going down shooting, in the dust of Nasiriyah.

"I can't do anything about that," she said. As for the rest of it, does anyone really wonder which she would rather have, a new toy in the mail or a time machine that could take her back to Lori so that she could tell her no, don't go, don't go with me to this war, don't die?

"I'd give four hundred billion dollars," she said. "I'd give anything."

The yellow ribbons in Wirt County hung first for Jessi remained, until they faded almost white, in remembrance of those soldiers still held captive after her rescue. When the 507th captives were returned, people here left the ribbons up, because it never seemed right to take them down. As the war changed into a deadly peace, with soldiers dying every day from sniper fire and bombers, it became clear that there might never be a right time.

"I got a gift," Dee Lynch said. "Not everyone did."

The house that had been a watchtower for a war became a shrine in the uneasy, bloody peace.

One day, an elderly man knocked at the door.

"Excuse me, sir, but is this the home of Jessica Lynch?" he asked.

Usually, state troopers manning the driveway turned curiosity seekers away, but there was something so earnest in this man that he was allowed through.

Jessi rolled from her bedroom.

"It is an honor I never could have dreamed of," he said, and a minute later he was gone.

A few nights later, around midnight, Jessi was lifted into her bed, with a photo album for company. Outside, the flags hung straight down in dead calm, and only the moths stirred the air as they fluttered around the porch light that was finally just right. The six-hundred-dollar dog, Cody, played dead again on the boards of the porch, and there was not one sound in the whole hollow except the singing of the insects and, from Jessi's room, sobs.

"She's lookin' at pictures of Lori, and crying," Greg Lynch said, his eyes red. Dee stood across the kitchen, staring at the tops of her shoes.

The physical therapy continued through

the summer and into the fall. In September, Jessie raised the American flag at a high school football game, and walked all the way across the kitchen.

In late September, she was honored by old soldiers in a ceremony at the V.F.W. The veterans made her a member for life, taking her young, smooth hands in old, shaking ones. They told her she was a hero, and they ought to know.

It is hard to say what Jessi will do when she can move without pain. She still wants to work with children, and she still very much wants what she calls "a normal life."

"I want to sit down and eat dinner with my husband, you know, normal stuff."

She has had songs written about her, and poems, and even interpretive dance pieces. Artists from all over the country painted portraits and did sketches of her face. But they all used the same model: the picture of Jessi and her camouflage cap, the flag behind her. It is the likeness that they love.

But Jessi will never be in camouflage again, unless she marches in a Veterans Day parade. The next time she hides it will be behind a veil, as she begins that normal life.

Twenty-nine

The Long Shadow of Jessica Lynch

Among the millions of photographs and video images taken during the odyssey of Jessica Lynch, one is a perfect metaphor for her legacy here in the mountains, and maybe beyond.

It is not the green-tinged, night-vision video of her being taken from Saddam Hussein General Hospital, or that first image of her face, stricken but trying to smile, as she was carried to a waiting helicopter.

It is not in the boxes of snapshots of beauty queen pageants, softball games and senior proms, not on the cover of *People* magazine, not in the newspaper photographs of her victorious ride through her hometown in the convertible, medals on her chest.

The photograph that best captured her story does not even include Jessi. It was taken near the courthouse steps in Elizabeth on April 1, during the wild celebration that followed her rescue.

The photograph, taken by Connie Dale and published in *The Parkersburg News* and *Sentinel*, shows a Wirt County firefighter in his yellow slicker and helmet, holding an American flag over his head.

One hand, his right, grips the flag's staff, and the other hand clutches the red and white stripes, pulling them tight. The face underneath is young, unsmiling. He stares straight ahead into the bright lights of the television cameras.

Looming behind and above him on the front of the courthouse is his shadow, in the shape of the young man but bigger, darker. It is two stories tall.

One is real, just an image of a brave young man, the kind of man who would run into a burning building — or maybe drive a truck across a desert into the middle of a war. It is a fine picture, a postcard for this place and its people.

The other image is larger, much larger, but it is only a trick of light.

Acknowledgments

I would like to thank the Lynch family, every last cousin, for their kindness and stories and hospitality in a difficult time. I would like to thank the people of West Virginia and the Ohio Valley for their patience and insights in shaping not just the story of Jessica, but the place that she is from. I would like to thank the Governor's Office of the State of West Virginia, for its help throughout this process, and especially Randy Coleman and Joe Carey for all they did — not for me but for the Lynch family. I'd like to thank everyone who swung a hammer or washed a dish at the Lynch house while I was there and for all the wonderful stories they told me when they stopped to take a breath.

I would like to thank my editor, Jordan Pavlin, who, for the second time, kept me from a nervous breakdown, and my agent, Amanda Urban, who, with the best possible intentions, almost gave me one. I'd like to thank Sonny Mehta for his faith in me, and Paul Bogaards for his advocacy. In general, I want to thank all the people at Knopf, not just for this book but also for others that I was also proud to be a part of. I would also like to thank the people of Louisiana and Alabama for being my friends, warts and all.

— *Rick Bragg*

We would like to thank everyone who took part in Jessi's rescue and recovery. We would like to extend a special thank you to the Iraqi citizens who aided Jessi, and to all the men and women of the armed services and Special Operations who helped in the rescue mission. We know we may never know your names, but we are proud of you. You are our heroes.

We'd like to give a special thanks to Corporal Regina Bacon for traveling from Kuwait and staying by Jessi's bedside during the whole ordeal.

Our thanks to the Heinz Corporation for giving us transportation to Germany; to Ken and Tammy Fisher and the Fisher Foundation for giving us a place to stay so we could be with our daughter; to Peter Anderson, Vivian Wilson and Kathy Gregory; to Governor Bob Wise and his entire staff; to Randy Coleman, Joe Carey and Mike Garrison; to Senator Jay Rockefeller; to the West Virginia State Troopers; and to the law enforcement personnel of Wirt County.

Our thanks go to Chief Warrant Officer Four Dana Kees, Major Mike Cadel and the West Virginia National Guard.

We'd also like to thank the doctors who treated Jessi in Iraq and the medical staff who treated Jessi at the field hospital.

And our thanks to Colonel Rubenstein, Dr. Tyler Putnam and Lieutenant Colonel Sally Harvey and the entire medical and nursing staff of Landstuhl Regional Medical Center; the Landstuhl MPs; Sergeant Forward, Sergeant Baker and Chaplain Hopkins.

Our thanks to General Kevin Kiley, Lieutenant Colonel Dr. Greg Argyros and the entire medical, nursing, physical therapy and psychology staff of Walter Reed Army Medical Center; and to Sergeant First Class

John Richter and the MPs at Walter Reed from Fort Meade, Fort Belvoir and Fort Myer.

Thanks also to Denise Hoover and Pat Kupfner; and to Greg Smith for making Jessi's first outing after coming home a success.

We'd like to express our appreciation to Burt Reed, Justin Eisenhofer and the staff of Mountain River Physical Therapy; and also to Lee Eastman, Kenly Webster, Steve Goodwin and Aly Goodwin Gregg.

A special thank you to the community of Wirt County and all the businesses and individuals who donated materials and equipment and who worked on the Jessi Home Project and especially to the families who gave up their time with the volunteers, so they could help us. We would like to thank every organization and everyone who prepared a meal and brought items to our household. Thanks to the family and friends who answered telephone calls and e-mails, handled the mail, took care of our personal business and most of all, a heartfelt thank you to everyone who said a prayer. Thank you to all the people who reached out to us from across the country and sent cards and money and gifts.

The prayers, love and support from everyone around the world are greatly appreciated.

We know we have forgotten names, but please believe us, your face and your contribution has not and will never be forgotten.

— *The Lynch family*

About the Author

Rick Bragg is the author of two best-selling books, Ava's Man *and* All Over but the Shoutin'. *He divides his time between New Orleans and his native Alabama.*